EVERY
WHERE
ALIEN

EVERY WHERE ALIEN

Brad Walrond

AMISTAD

An Imprint of HarperCollinsPublishers

HarperCollins books may be purchased for educational, business, or sales promotional use. For information, please email the Special Markets Department at SPsales@harpercollins.com.

In Association with Moore Black Press.

FIRST EDITION

Designed by THE COSMIC LION

Illustrations by Tim Nottage.

Bird image on pages 91 to 97 © Sandi/stock.adobe.com.

Library of Congress Cataloging-in-Publication Data has been applied for.

ISBN 978-0-06-337799-8

24 25 26 27 28 LBC 5 4 3 2 1

Moore Black Press is the press for the radical Black imagination.

We are forging the future of poetry at the highest level
and cultivating the unexpected and the beautiful new.

mooreblackpress.com

For

Mom
May she be proud and beaming up there

and

Pep and Zook: Frantz Simpson and Craig Davis
my muse, my brothers in life, art, friendship, and transition

and

for every being who will have need of a dream to save them
Dreams belong to the future; find yourself there, no matter what

Contents

HOME CHURCH: HOW HOUSE MAKES A HOME

MANHOOD: A BOY'S CALCULUS

JOURNEY: A SHAMAN'S NARCOTIC

MOOD: HERE FOR THE HEREAFTER

EPILOGUE.

Foreword

Dear Aliens Every Where,

This is NOT a test.

Welcome to the brilliant work of my dear brother, and fellow poet, Brad Walrond. I warmly call him "My Baldwin." I first found his spiritual work in the form of poetry and movement at a gathering hole for poets and artists called Frank's in the roaring '90s. A bar downstairs, a circled-up safe space for poets, lovers, dancers, twenty-something-year-old trouble makers, and future torch bearers of the culture. *The Sunday Tea Party.* It was black hippie and new renaissance bustling, and Brad was an audience favorite.

A bright child of Gotham, Brad's poems force readers to snap out of the collective amnesia of an American dream and confront the reality of who we be and where we will ultimately end up if we don't find ways to outwrite, outwit, and outlive oppression.

Brad's poems become a humanitarian extension, a necessary limb stretching and moving through time, gliding across dark dance floors, carrying us into the only embryonic safe place. A community protected by poets, a language midwifed through middle passage memories and the necessity of black joy. His work is the poetic cartography of a body mapped perfectly among the stars. You have to look up to find them.

I am so happy I found him,

again.

To be
EVERYWHERE.

And
ALIEN.

Is to be black in America.

This book is a balm for the wounded and a testimony for the forgotten.
A light bearer in a world surrounded by shadows. Walrond's poems are a
blues only a student of Baraka could hum in time. Proof of life when we are
attempting to simply keep our heads above water. A Jesus crown for Kalief
Browder. Walrond's work finds ways to float peacefully. Back flat against the
waves, pulling us like a lullaby onto an unforgiving foreign soil. Somehow,
still, finding a house music classic song in the tide.

Outbursts of laughter, break beats as lines, the reader becomes immersed in
an ongoing journey of self discovery as they travel/read. He's a meticulous
craftsman, studied and well versed, yet his poems are uncontained like a holy
ghost on the page.

A book of freedom plow poems. A remembrance and a reckoning. A needle
against the record.

Perhaps, a small time machine. Life support for a new Harlem. The ghosts of
St. Nich Pub parade in unison joining the Lenox Lounge choir of angels for

the book signing. This sermon, bursting through the juke joint speakers, is a calling from the outhere.

A portal to an exquisite afro future.
A future where Walrond "comes for" Picasso
Masking his familiarity with black magic.

He writes:

Hieroglyphs are not Hallucinations—

A book of masterful poems exploding with love despite pain.

In "How to Describe a Slave Ship in Three Minutes or Less,"
the irony and wit of Walrond is beautifully pronounced.

"genocide obviously america's first opioid crisis

uncontrolled substances take the name Harriet
controlled substances grandfathered in

how did we all get here?
without a moral compass.

       Where are we?

That's right a slave ship

5 4 3 2 1."

Alien, we are
even when home.

What an extreme honor to publish these deserving words.

My dear friend, who was witness in 1997 when Moore Black Press was
becoming a voice for the next wave of black poets creating the new black
canon.

We courageously create our own indelible time stamp,
Writing, dancing, shouting ourselves into existence.

We continue.

We every

        where.

Alien.

To the future,

jessica Care moore
Publisher, Poet, Moore Black Press

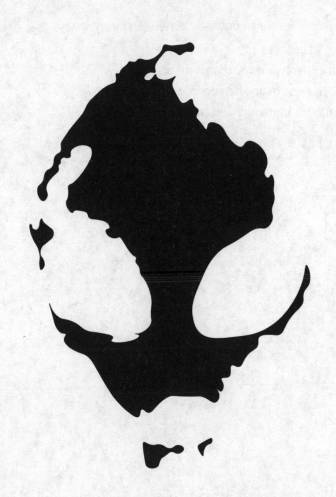

"The battle involves more than a mere
altruistic interest in an alien people.
It is a battle for humanity and human culture."

—W. E. B. DU BOIS

PROLOGUE.

THE UNTITLED, THE UNNAMED, & THE UNNAMEABLE

Earth born a Mother too pregnant
too free for this settler's world:

> "On the island of Manhate, and its environs,
> there may well be four or five hundred men of
> different sects and nations: the Director General
> told me that there were men of eighteen
> different languages; they are scattered here and there
> on the river, above and below, as the
> beauty of and convenience of the spot has invited
> each to settle: some mechanics, however, who
> ply their trade, are ranged under the fort; all the others
> are exposed to the incursions of the natives, who
> in the year 1643, while I was there, actually killed some
> two score Hollanders, and burnt many houses and barns
> full of wheat."
> —*Father Isaac Jogues, 3 August 1646*

Natives?

how sweet Father Jogues's politesse seasons the heinous history
the Dutch West India Company digests inside its Christian mob.

Indigenous | Native | Savage
Native | Savage | Indigenous

syllables fell together their found art.
a diphthong collage bioengineered for Father Isaac
Jogues's morning meditations harden like scripture

into sour apple–flavored Jolly Ranchers
cloying civilized tongues apart from their conscience.

As if somehow the mere
Acknowledgement of: *"the Locals"*

—that hipster's vernacular dipped
ever so quickly in its own conceit—

doubles as an absolution bled of crimes
Directors' General hush against humanity like a hoard.

How else might words like genocide & ethnic cleansing
ferret so glib in and out of a fur trader's mouth?
as if the beaver is indigenous to everywhere else
besides Nieuw Amsterdam?

Indigenous | Native | Savage
Native | Savage | Indigenous

Taste like friction, don't it? Peel it back. Suck.
Taste how corn syrup never reverts to maize or maple.

Too late—fuck! Native:
a word meant to be an untold story
blasts its undead offspring at the back of your mouth.

How come no one ever asks first?

if you like to swallow

a word | too fertile

for a settler's memory of his own genocidal hand
cocked like Fort Amsterdam at the back of your head.

how feckless a nation

will rewrite what it already forgot
ink the amnesia it must rehearse. As if

the Walloons & the Hollanders are the progenitors
of organic produce and not *"the savages*
who had formerly cleared the ground"

how the minister the blacksmith the miller
the fur trader the bailiff the mason and
the patron's agent never can quite   recall

how an inheritance contrabands into a Trail of Tears
when one un-remembers from whom it came.

> "This colony is composed of about a hundred persons,
> who reside in some twenty-five or thirty houses built
> along the river, as each found most convenient. . . .
> The forest furnishing many large pines, they make boards
> by means of their mills, which they have here

for this purpose. They found some pieces of ground all ready,
which the savages had formerly cleared, and in which they
sow wheat and oats for beer, and for their horses. . . .
Trade is free to all; this gives the Indians all things cheap,
each of the Hollanders outbidding his neighbor,
and being satisfied provided he can gain some little profit."

Farm-to-table? I wonder who invented that.

How much longer must we pretend
they taught us how to recycle?

Ingest their Napa Valley compost as if it were candy?

Without ever asking: is this?
what sour apples taste like—in the wild;

I mean the savage ones, the native ones,

the indigenous apples, the earth so immaculately
conceived of her own lovemaking

long long before Jolly Rancher could remember not to forget
the atrocities buried in the groundwater
of his own barbarian name?

Indigenous | Native | Savage

words candied too sweet for their own gruel.

GOTHAM: WHERE THE KIDS RAISE THEMSELVES

THE INDIGENOUS

balls deep inna da Flatbush Extension
we was born again inside a Jacob Lawrence painting
North of da Mason-Dixon Line

Jan Rodrigues the Dominican love child
of a Portuguese sailor and an African woman

is the first verifiable non-Indian to take up residence
on Manhattan Isle

    somehow no word obtains for a world
    of melanin-scarred babies conceived at the back door of consent

Who then are the Natives?
The Ones who give the boroughs its staples?
The Lenape who slash and burn?
The Ones they slashed and burned?

whose offerings we remember
their sacrifice wont to forget

cushaw squash | rabbit | beaver
prickly pear | popped amaranth | epazote oil
smoked cottonwood leaf quail | yucca fruit
bitter acorn | blue corn | and bear root

Domino Sugar | Greg Tate | Junior's cheesecake
Ray's famous pizza | roti, j'ouvert | & the Puerto Rican
Day Parade | maduros | Black Rock Coalition
matzo ball | pastrami & | hot corn soup

Sweet Mother of God, Madonna does not know how to vogue.

sidewalks echolocate
eggshell Adidas &
beatbox cheekbones.

Wu-Tang | Vernon Reid | Living Colour | Tamara,
Sandra St. Victor, Sophia Ramos | The Family Stand | Patti Smith,
Biggie Smalls | Soulsonic Force | tables turn, whip
R & B | ABBA, Afrobeat & | the conga into stiff peaks
dub beats | break rock | in a Paradise Garage

Larry Levan's dance floor wraps concrete
round its rhythm
iron horses teeter-totter & screech
with high-gloss hormones in heat

postpubescent | seesaw
quick rich traps | rough landings

ambition correlate with rent parties
Slow money run the Wall Street Laundromat

pockets pick

the hard-won grit oiled into Afros
red-lit inflated egos of would-be matadors

the air down here is a freestyle cypher
streaming lyrics onto the droplets of Mother's dreams

the three train is a river.

run free in Brooklyn
fed every day by the blood of living and dead
gods' daughters and sons.

dreams wet with want perish the Future

Every day . . .

THE GODFATHER'S TENURE

"It's time to make America safe again. It's time to make America one again. I know it can be done because I did it by changing New York City from 'the crime capital of America' to according to the FBI the safest large city in America. What I did for New York City, Donald Trump will do for America."

—Rudolph Giuliani

Enter into evidence the blood-let IV Amendment:

The right of the people to be secure in their persons, houses, papers, and effects, against unreasonable searches and seizures, shall not be violated. . . .

1994 Police Commissioner William Bratton's
elite Street Crimes Unit:

plain-cloth pigs in unmarked cars promulgate

STOP > **FRISK** > SWARM > EXECRATE > PULL OUT > MOLEST

Become the NYPD's religious reenactment
of SCOTUS's *Terry v. Ohio* (1968) "reasonable suspicion"

SWARM > **STOP** > **FRISK** > EXECRATE > MOLEST > PULL OUT

New Yawk's b-boy train gang, bars
spit-bomb spray-painted verbs in cypher

Latin Kings, leprechauns, sag-pant Nuyorican
Christopher Street, punk rock, goth, Red Alert

Black purple silver glitter lipstick
track the musk of the living

Below the poverty line

SWARM > EXECRATE > **STOP** > **FRISK** > MOLEST > PULL OUT

club: a Shelter housing the dispossessed
along the rhythms of the 3rd rail

kids bump tuck and toke
they ecstasy with communion

even among the fallen *Angel* officiating
The Limelight club's Evensong

SWARM > EXECRATE > MOLEST > **STOP** > **FRISK** > PULL OUT

New York City's underground
cld not escape the divine laws.

the courts expunge near half
the Street Crimes Unit gun cases

for being false arrests
                              inasmuch
as they were also true.

SWARM > EXECRATE > MOLEST > PULL OUT > **STOP** > **FRISK**

drones dispatch in service of Mayor Giuliani's
adolescent locker-room grope for illegal firearms

STOP > **FRISK** > SWARM > EXECRATE > PULL OUT > MOLEST

In the black of night
In the black of day

a whole city sequestered to
the blue-ball quest for black steel

wired cut & uncut
circumcised & uncircumcised

SWARM > **STOP** > **FRISK** > EXECRATE > MOLEST > PULL OUT

documented & undocumented
to the furtive movements of brown bodies

SWARM > EXECRATE > **STOP** > **FRISK** > MOLEST > PULL OUT

until the early morning of February 4, 1999
in the Soundview section of the Bronx

when a 22-year-old immigrant's cigarette-lit devout shadow
holograms a front stoop into a killing field

SWARM > EXECRATE > MOLEST > **STOP** > **FRISK** > PULL OUT

14

at the shooting range: what do we call the black cropped figure?

a wallet and a pager
bait & switch alters

a refugee's twitch prelude to a deadly kiss

in less than two minutes
six syllables string like a high-wire act

between the room share & the club
between Guinea & the South Bronx

Am   a   dou   Di   al   lo

become an echo chamber
of 41 could-have-been-me bullets

the one (African) mother's child
even the club kids can't dance out of their minds

SWARM > EXECRATE > MOLEST > PULL OUT > **STOP** > **FRISK**

succumbed to the Funk
lost & found in suspended gestation.

we dressed in layers & margins
Mass incarcerated & falsely accused

pending the decades-long thrashing against the NYPD
waterboard stoking the Godfather's brand

STOP > **FRISK** > SWARM > EXECRATE > PULL OUT > MOLEST

the tatted, the rat-tat-tat, become the rebel pulse
denied Gotham exequy.

Our DNA mapped onto CBGB's nucleotides
vinyl hid in pleural places and resolved never to be out-punked

SWARM > **STOP** > **FRISK** > EXECRATE > MOLEST > PULL OUT

grunge house rock acid jazz trudge
long and hard for the groove

SWARM > EXECRATE > **STOP** > **FRISK** > MOLEST > PULL OUT

hardly noticed the time.
Survival

SWARM > EXECRATE > MOLEST > **STOP** > **FRISK** > PULL OUT

was the only memory
steeling our desecrated unbent spine.

———————————

SWARM > EXECRATE > MOLEST > PULL OUT > **STOP** > **FRISK**
SWARM > EXECRATE > MOLEST > **STOP** > **FRISK** > PULL OUT
SWARM > EXECRATE > **STOP** > **FRISK** > MOLEST > PULL OUT
SWARM > **STOP** > **FRISK** > EXECRATE > MOLEST > PULL OUT
STOP > **FRISK** > SWARM > EXECRATE > PULL OUT > MOLEST

DOWNTOWN NILE

September 11, 2001.
A stone's throw boom-
erangs precisely where
America's collective
un-memory **ground
to Zero**. denial been
run right through that
African American Bu-
rial Ground contemp-
oraneously housed in
Ted Weiss Federal
Building @ 290 B'way
where 419 Africans—
most slave some free,
buried as the 18th
century turned—have
now **come to rest**
in Lower Manhattan's
Civic Center **no less**
than 15,000 Negroes
interred, on six acres
behind God's back
when New York City
had earned its ivory

privilege as the na-
tion's 2nd largest
slaveholder. Is it any
wonder this Ted Weiss
Federal Building @
290 B'way occupies
Wall Street & the
World Trade Center's
synapse? those
Windows on Our World
a foregone conclusion.
Collect a history that
could only be Ours.
The window washers
survived *how* the hu-
mans have managed
to carve our common
ancestor into castes
of continents and déjà
vus. **Flash! Bang!
Pray!** Gotham's pre-
history not too modern
for a miracle. **!Terror!**
Will our panes to shatter
when they touch. **Re-
discover?** Our likeness
among the shards

THIS KIND GENTRY

1.

A black marker, a redline, and a Reconstruction
banks fly in the gentry from all kinds of places.
bright new neighbors have been loaned their
happiness at low interest rates. JPMorgan
Chase; all the niggers' deed into quicksand.
Community board members, born amortized,
pasteurize fresh. Revitalization signals the rescue
effort already transitioned into a Recovery.

2.

The Indigent, the Sentient, the Methadone
Clinic, I promise, will one day return for a cleansing;
at Harlem's African American Day Parade
the Progenitors advance the Scouts first.
A majorette, a drum line, a Vision
knew: Only chance to save Harlem
now is in her bare-head magic.

3.

gem-feminine incantation see through
the impervious amongst us; infrared bird's-
eye portrait of the indigo wound leased to

us all. cover the unrecovered beneath a Brooklyn
Moon, the gods consecrate at Sunday Tea.
our #Heaven must be earthbound now

4.

lest we all perish inside a Whole Foods
antiseptic swarm on 125th and Lenox Ave.
a little Red Rooster wolf-howls from the North side
of the bay: that clapboard Lounge may be the
only portal we have Left.

PABLO THE AFROFUTURIST

Anyanwu Takes Over Picasso's Tumblr Feed

1.

A filthy room in a Paris museum
become a portal to the afterworld;

      that mere collection of masks
      masked by the unuttered weight of corpuscles
      oiled into their untold stories

a wonder there was

any room in there

for him at all

Culture scrubbed of its blood
Craft denied the metaphysics of form
Africa excised of its bodies

Pablo felt it—the crucible of being watched;
knew the instant his witness made him an accomplice
to corporal rites denied their Fetish

Qu'est-ce que c'est   plus savage   que la Modernité?
Enter into evidence Picasso's   mucid hands at Trocadéro

He—crowned at the Catalan brothel, beneath

Les Demoiselles d'Avignon—

the apotheosis of L'Art Moderne

Imagine! How annals of knowledge, expunged of sources, can be transcribed,
by way of the terror rattling Picasso's bones

nearly pissed his pants
in that mundunugu shrine
to black magic.

Pablo knew somewhere in Abaddon
there was a word for this—

the feeling of the whole Color
of a continent disemboweled.

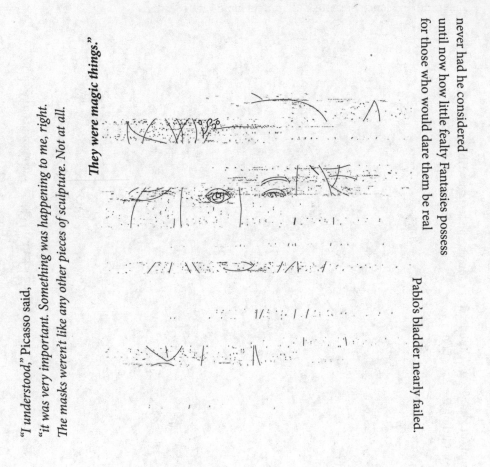

never had he considered
until now how little fealty Fantasies possess
for those who would dare them be real

They were magic things.

Pablo's bladder nearly failed.

"I understood," Picasso said,
"it was very important. Something was happening to me, right.
The masks weren't like any other pieces of sculpture. Not at all.

*"When I went to the Trocadéro,
it was disgusting. The flea market,
the smell. I was alone. I wanted to
get away, but I didn't leave."*

By God we've got to
give Pablo credit.
In his own words
he stayed.

2.

What else is language
Beside a nascent form of turrets?
The conscious itch—chicken's scratch
become words like Kemet & Co-opt.
Quantum & Kush as the ashened third eyes
in the Omo Valley

Hieroglyphs are not Hallucinations—
they Hologram the Early Universe
melanate the trace evidence
of a unified theory

Funny how punctuation convey so much meaning

History never concedes the facts:
Picasso's genius came of age
in his first "Negro period"

23

The European's only Original Thought
is to subject the savage to its pen.

"African art?" Pablo Picasso says,
he "Never heard of it!" —

Louder explanations do not appease
the absence of reason

Picasso?!
Et tu, Brute?

had such *"a profound identity of spirit with
the tribal peoples, as well as a generalized
assimilation of the principles and character of their art"*

Picasso You?

who, according to William Rubin, the renowned curator of the
New York City Museum of Modern Art (1984) exhibit,
*"PRIMITIVISM" in 20th Century Art:
Affinity of the Tribal and the Modern*

Never ?

Heard of ?

words run on mad without their meaning
Eve's hallucinations have syllables
No Period.   Began her life's sentence.

No Period.   Began her life's sentence.

It ?

3.

Pyramids & Placentas show their proofs
Life can never be artificial!

Blindness of Color never makes for honest art.

Picasso!

Truth—like the genome—
has a pigment.

All those masks have faces

26

HOW TO DESCRIBE A SLAVE SHIP
IN THREE MINUTES OR LESS

all the drinks are vinegar and virgin
sweetened with loads of cane sugar and cotton

a Caribbean cruise loops in a vine GIF
Pile 'Em In! All Aboard!

each ticket cost freedom

press like | hit send
retweet | screen grab | it does not matter

this mission | accept or not | will self-destruct | in 5 4 3 2 1

this image is a superpredator.
this image is a mass incarcerated.

this image passes

Go

with or without college
degrees or mortgages.

it does not matter
this image purchases prisons for hotels

picture a microaggression stutters
on the word: infinite

imagine being Colored
blind in Mississippi

imagine a murder of crows fly south inside a dog-whistle

a 20th Century
sly as a fox

relativity is partial to light
grim on darkness

all the theories are white.
all the facts are black.

feather and tar fraternize a Universe
born dark invisible and expanding

imagine: an owner, an amnesiac,
a sociopath, and a citizen, are synonyms

painting the Barclays Center clear
as a Homestead Act

the glass windows are ceilings;
everything hangs so nice.

strange fruit are bats
bruising America's heirlooms

if only we were good enough
to live the lives of our antiquities

in the Sainsbury Africa Galleries
of the British Museum

over 200,000 objects lie in wait
as if they are black.

if only we were royal enough

for those Congolese artifacts King Leopold II
ferreted into Belgium

patents wait so patient
in his Royal Museum of Central Africa

there it is: imagine

A slave ship as a Royal Museum happy at sea

while Africa's remains center at the back of the bus
remembering nothing besides possession.

Imagine every ship is a corporation
Imagine every corporation got a jones for whitewash

Imagine a brand is the cleanest
most effective form of forgetting

which color does what to whom
after all the dirty minerals spit bath.

Imagine the West, as oneword,
chronicles the advent of cognitive dissonance.

while Eckhart Tolle's New Age
wipes space-time white as snow

rare Earths warm just how you like it;
a wet womb—a blank check.

all borders, no boundaries.
gateway drugs read better as constitutions

genocide obviously America's first opioid crisis

uncontrolled substances take the name Harriet
controlled substances grandfathered in

how did we all get here?
without a moral compass.

    Where are we?

That's right a slave ship

5 4 3 2 1.

VINTAGE FUTURE

1.

the kisses we remember,
remember us first.

at 90% water most pronouns suffer
from inexperience

i fish for the *human* beings

ocean floor of club Le Boy, Copacabana, Rio de Janeiro
discovered a freestyle samba,
homeless, in my waist

each step velcro & wet
took to *hers*

we transgendered

embodied a language
shot hot from the hip

we did not speak until we swallowed
the same tongue in the upstairs bathroom.

2.

i

have grown
up in New York
City Michelin-star
Kitchens where man-
ners are never welcome
to dinner. Chefs
have thrown bowls
at my head then *ask-*
ed me to leave. my
blood line piques of
Scotch bonnet from
the Caribbean Sea.
the fish fly after they
walk on the water
down there—i. did.
not! Leave. cast-iron
beneath a high-noon
sun, protest is my birth-
right sculpted out of
stone. are you fuckin'
stupid, why? should i
have to pronounce a
sentence like "do not
throw a bowl at my head
unless you have thought
through all the damned
consequences." my ivy league
education not withstanding
most niggers bleed negro.
plus ivy league sucks dick—
and not that well. u want me?!
to suck your dick. Oui! Chef i thought this
was what we were already doing. i will show you
how it is done—with abandon. leave you, post hoc,
to your unrivaled vices; teachable moments oblige no
follow-up conversation. water is a Master denominator.
black and white cum   out in the wash

3.

why
?
all this so-called progress to color tv

ain't we
?
stuck in syndication inside an analog american dream

i pray the fantasy ends with a strong wi-fi signal
and no need for a wire hanger

antennae, kisses!
see you at the end of the show.

DESIRE:
THE GOD'S
MOST NATURAL
EXPERIMENT

I GET LIFTED OH

we did not choose each other
on that underground Wednesday night
Harlem dance floor.
We were   *chosen*

hearts sweated like rain
smiles crackling the fire spit across
our language barrier
we found ourselves in   *anthem*

instinct on spin cycle: knee, washing board, tongue
spliced cross 12 inches of a spirit-filled
I Get Lifted Oh /
I Get Lifted Yes   *house song*

a juke joint east of Lenox Lounge
become a pop-up lion's den stage right
of the dance floor; frot hands hung
to the top side of the table   *hunting*

like pheromones of spontaneously combusted
paramours. time lost and barely, barely found
I remember next. I do not remember
before coat check

and a train ride   *north*
and an address I called home

and a passion felt like God and Sun
primordial hot three-letter words

                              gateway

to Four. we tattooed ourselves lips-first
to the front door the morning sun an elbow
prodding us together and apart; a part
together as we tried to not leave against

                              our will.

SCORE

A Sonnet Turnt Out on the Low

Pull up, no tag, no rules. Exploit, low light, eye bait, lasers
come magnets. / The ardent hunt for consent, in the hot rod,
hazard light, and the half / unbuckled pant waist. The denizens
flood the movie house: arms, gambits / spent Black & Milds,
poppers, Christian Dior cologne, lube. Men blame for gaff /
they would never have asked for. Touched, tugged, belonged to
needs requiring mouths / to confess in the absence of scripture
and speech. Backs hold, nipples tuft / somewhere between
want and murmur. The OG, the new brand, the down south,
/ the wild-card peacock, the new issue. Lift hoods, switch
gears, oils change, seats buff. / Chasses bend, buckle, bruise,
and replace. Day Trade, doormen, church queens, the *gworls* /
frat brothers, hoodrats, middle sons, bitch niggas, construction
workers, bow / out uniforms, suspend their claims, abandon
titles, to wives, deeds, worlds. / Heads bow where penance
begs in braille. Sesame opens, seed disavows / all priors. '80s
porn, pantomime, soundtrack. A chorus loses score. / Rides
the staccato against the back wall filled with late matinee lore.

I DO NOT SPEAK LATIN

aye -aye   -aye-   aye

ee -ee   -ee   -ee   -eeee

ohhhhhhh ohhhhhhh

     Damn!

ooooooh!   oooooooh! OOOOOOh!

   Damn You!

Who? embezzled all the LGBTQ vowels.
Who? pays these Latin-minders

to card my sex
track my browser history

The patriarchs, and cult leaders, and hired priests
dispatch cogs of middle school librarians.

herd the sapiens into their lonely
wormwood boxes.

i shook 'em in the straights
while on the hunt for fresh game

my lovers *god* the subversive;
at our zenith

gender and binaries go YHWH,
and unpronounced.

desire and friction favorite their own superpositions.
In my Universe the vowels know how

set themselves on fire
find themselves a room

little bit a space
just enough time.

1986: AN ELEGY FOR OUR COLDEST WAR

Commemorating Gay Men of African Descent's (GMAD's)
30th Year Anniversary and the Legacy of Black Gay Men
Organizing in Response to Homophobia, Racism, and
the HIV/AIDS Pandemic

1.

Could be The Ballroom was always our nuclear option
a rock scrabble bunker become a threshing floor.
how we survived our Coldest War

a mother a father an entire house full of babies
tucked into mangers woven out of street-corner filament
limber enough to parent those of us:

born with and without parents
with and without islands

begat inside flags with and without stripes
while reading for A-level exams

stretched astride empires and Queens
too black to be British

too gay to be queer—
too poor for the crowns we deserve.

2.

Boys and girls born beyond signage
onto intersections above and below 42nd Street
where hormones traffic themselves

run all the rules busts all the lights
come shot out of blackness too Pentecostal
for its own beneficence

Could be the ballroom scene laid its own bedrock
atop an inference; as if by subterfuge.
as if by stagecraft as if by premonition:

the way | we live
the way | we die
the way | we transition

in and out of space
in and out of time

in and out   of academies & boarding schools
with and without degrees.

in and out of dimension
the lives we all span   is a performance.

3.

1986: What a performance it was!
In the year of our Lord June 30, 1986
adjudicating case 478 U.S. 186

otherwise known as *Bowers v. Hardwick*
the Supreme Court upheld Georgia's
sodomy laws in a 5-4 decision.

This year 1986 according to dissenting Justice
Harry A. Blackmun—enjoined by William J. Brennan Jr.,
Thurgood Marshall, and John Paul Stevens—

our nation's highest court
became obsessively focused on homosexual activity

So happens this same year 1986
a midsummer night's dream is bequeathed
to Reverend Charles Angel.

a new faith begins its practice inside the
living rooms of black gay men

fagged playing Russian roulette with their secrets
the waters break:

Gay Men of African Descent is born.

June 14, 1986: Daniel Garrett freebases on a
James Baldwin line: *"Our history is each other"*

and a group of black gay men exhale
enough pride inside a writer's workshop

to inscribe themselves
a new nation: *Other Countries*

write themselves out of a BlackHeart collecting the
floodlit life force condensed inside Joseph's Beam

in some ways we all still live huddled,
impatient, un-relented inside Joseph's hologram

If There's a Cure for This I Don't Want It

October 1986
Craig Harris black gay living
with AIDS and walking realness

grabs the mic from San Francisco's health commissioner
at the American Public Health Association's first AIDS workshop
speaking for all of us he proclaims: "I Will Be Heard!"

before Craig's mic drops
National Minority AIDS Council
is born

Craig Harris | Paul Kawata | Gil Gerard
Suki Ports | Marie St. Cyr

invite our colored selves to the Ball
because the rainbow was never   enough.

4.

On this runway Audre Lorde cries *Dear Joe*
& *the tinny jukebox music comes up through the floor of our shoes*

This runway is a Battle!
This runway is an Extravaganza!

Watch | Listen | Learn!
This Battle Is and Is Not Yours

The Old Way | The New Way.

Either way spells perseverance
crafted out of imaginary high school diplomas

The Old Way | The New Way

Either way spells perseverance out of
nothing besides our poverty our dis/ease,

our sex | our privilege
our death | our shame

a people | a culture | an art form | a wellspring is born.

5.

When life spans splinter into foreshortened seasons
a phallus-engorged pandemic goes jackhammer & rogue
sometimes God opens   the second door

1986 is a second door
a portal in time manned by the Queens
of the Damned

a Middle Passage collects itself onto dry ground
An ADODI river collapses alongside a
New York City Nile

Shamans sing:
in & out | of gender.
in & out | of place. Yoruba priests

walk Bizarre.

6.

When My Brother Fell

I cared not how rich he was
how Caribbean he was

how Ivy League his poison oak
how much Southern fruit pickled his veins

When My Brother Fell

I cared not how many Prospect Park trees
bear witness to his lovemaking. I paid no attention

to which butch-queen-voguing-fem
he was fucking in between bushes

or to how big | how thick
how heavy | the thorns

he let ride his back into Heaven

When My Brother Fell
I picked up his weapons and never questioned

the category he walked
how much makeup he had on

or which label *she* wore
behind closed doors

I never questioned if?
his momma knew. If?

his daddy cared
I

kept
walking.

7.

Essex said, *"There was no one lonelier than you, Joseph"*

30 years later, we not gon' do it that way this time
The Ballroom collapses whole classes into nations

Every call gets a response
every name   every category
every non-binary   is an intention

A Universal law makes its own rules
divines its own boundaries
causing legends to be born

While Paris burns

Assotto's Saints &
Willi's Ninjas stand guard

a whole river of boys born without bones
boys born without spoons let alone silver

bright boys born on islands in between boroughs
that rupture beneath their saltwater promise

Somehow The Ballroom always knew why
boys and girls born too fluid for homes

need Houses!
Essex said,   *"If we must die on the*
Front line don't let loneliness
kill us"

If There's a Cure for This I Don't Want It

1986 1986 1986 is: a house song   at morning mass
a break beat | a beat box | a carol

a love song | a dirge | a Brooklyn Children's Museum
born again | inside

a Donald Woods forest

1986

is a GMAD, an NMAC, an ADODI
a god-accented Ebonic

surviving for Joseph, for Essex, for Donald
for Willi, for Assotto Saint, for Craig Harris

For all Us born survivors of the Coldest War
with and without parents.

Born | too gay | too queer | for the crowns we deserve.

UNDER CONSTRUCTION

A Duplex

Flecked paint, an abstract, on determined thighs
She steered clear of these calloused dungarees

    side-eye, catfish my calloused dungarees?,
    the quick-eyed tease held fast to her freedoms.

bucks snare easy-quick inside them hurried freedoms
joe, poppy seed, buttah round as mornin'.

    street-style cosplay rounds out any mornin'
    how my lox managed to snag in her cream

Popeyes on the corner. Olive, cakes, cream, cheese!
baked fresh outta Brklyn, hot bagel cart

    Brklyn summers bake. Food carts cool enough.
    Where the workers grub, fresh rub can be found

Pick up jobs, hunger, they find each other
In the cash crops between construction sights.

USB

memories make for good wingmen

plug-in port to trouble

his muscle does not tread lightly

rattled me whole into a rag

abandoned at da side of da bed

left me for joy

picking up our pieces.

PHOTOJOURNALIST

For Shreya

1.

Eve mines her own mitochondria from Cave 13B
—the headland at Pinnacle Point overlooking the
Indian Ocean's Mossel Bay—

to propagate a kind she will never quite
be given credit for. Who'd have known the
eating of shellfish @ the Southern tip of Africa

on one summer day somewhere
between 170,000 and 40,000 years ago
would culture modern palates

out of negroid tongue; bloom humanity
out of leftover hominid, gristle, and bone.

seem the Earth's past, for its foreseeable future,
will: start and stop & start and stop
right here in the land of the San

where Eve must have lived the good life
atop the earliest evidence of human-worked
silcrete stone—a *bard* perhaps

foretelling the steel concrete-jungle
a rabid species will soon enough call home.
her eyes photojournal the rise and fall

of entire kingdoms in truncated windows of time
the black on Eve's face is and is not paint.
Intuition, ochre-sheer as a newfound shawl

drapes round consciousness's Dawn and lays
bare the omen bellowed across creation:
Eve must make herself ready for aeons of war.

      2.

1970, Bengali expatriates unmoor from one of
civilization's cradles. A woman from Kolkata, her
Dalit husband from Gangarampur.

They wear on the immigrant chain bound to Jackson Heights.
Two brilliant daughters belong to their futures. A brood collects
inside a stateless wish:

Escape the necrosis imbued to castes no karma
could ever choose; sluff the forceps even Darwin and
Gandhi had solder-clamped to their brow.

reprise any *sharanagati* into the absolution of a song.

Concrete jungle where dreams are made of /
There's nothing you can't do, now you're in New York

four blocks of refugee settlement in
Jackson Heights, carves an Adivasi outpost
ever under siege. an ingrown nail,

pincered to tradition, digests the poor as dharma.
this *New* World Black with its own nouveau-caste
too-American rules incline to leave unrecognized

these carbon-sure mtDNA descendants of Eve

3.

Ma's only Protection requires she map
these four blocks better than you do.
She knows only times of day

that 74th Street alleyway

—the one with the
5 o'clock shadow below the
busted streetlight facing the bodega—

shaves into a bridge over troubled water.

　　Womyn
earth-rich | dirt-poor
born knowin' how

to make any 13B flat, point toward:
Home. curve hot-iron ardor round
barrios of people crushed pavement.

shrimp and curry power the trenches
of an urban sprawl. sun-cauterized flesh
tenders comfort & warm.

Eve slither when she walk;
Ma! wet nurse the whole earth
in the valley of her hips.

contused hearts un-break over
& over in her umbilical hands!

WAR OF THE DRONES

best lovers are hacks;
patient determined meticulous

fire walls and graffiti bombs
inspire their own transgressions

we code in open source in Gotham
share only the retroviruses

interborough corporal commune

sidewalk peep show surveillance
satellite Tekserve on 23rd Street

at Chelsea's edge
where most apples bite or bottom

1 and 2s go good with
zeros and ones and threesomes

zero is the beginning of everything
the absence of secrets and power is freedom

Google is the last failed democracy—
United Nations is always in session

u can feed the whole world
on Twitter Grindr Tumblr Tinder Instagram

    where naked is the new normal
    avatars concuss and forget how

to reach out and touch / somebody's hand
make this world a better place / if you can

    hyperspace has already been colonized
    in the outer boroughs

we the only humans left
in the shadows of the Sun

    face-to-face we will save Earth from the Drones!

YEMAYA'S WINGS

chinned to an icon Mami split me too.
tongue stir Creole in river clay and salt water

Everything takes shape. Everything holds water.
Olokun holds everyone else born in between

up and down the coast sandbars perform their sanctuary
new rites rinse god-awful deeds into verse and nursery rhyme

Fresh fish and new coral make their appraisals of shipwreck
and heartbreak; as if to barter their regenerative opportunities

the whole hope of a village comes out to meet her. Our
Madre Agua, Yemojá, Yemanjá, Iemanjá, Nossa Senhora

Offerings gestate in the shallows
until our gills fashion for lovemaking

a duck, a tamale, a polysemy, a shrimp stew,
insists rapids submit eventually. we are the Occasion

they've come out to sea. took the risk
in middle storm to rediscover middle-earth.

the rain, the clouds! they will not cover us
we will need an Orisha for safe passage

Mami womb me your secret. collect the formless in your arms.
Mariners take up your orders from Yemaya's wings.

HOME CHURCH: HOW HOUSE MAKES A HOME

LIBATION PARTY NYC @ THE SULLIVAN ROOM

Resident DJ Ian Friday; Hosted by ManChild
Black and Afro Mosaic Soul

what happens in that DJ booth? why do it feel like dem dey dat spin dem
spirits arrive endowed with crates and crates of autoerotic instruments?
i came in on the low unannounced at 2 a.m., paid my damage at the door,
and thought—for sure—i would have time to find a spot to put my
knapsack down. the instant i stepped in front of the speaker the damned
Devil licked me in the ear with a white-coal Josh Milan mix of Nina
Simone's "I Put a Spell on You." underneath, i could hear Sade's
"Shelter Me," the David Morales version peeking through. i pushed
forward feeling my way along the right-side wall.

the dance floor gives like matted earth at the edge of a bayou—the parquet
planks anoint with a voudon paste of sweat, baby powder, incense, and ash.
dammit! tonight i thought for sure i needed the Holy Ghost first. DJ had
other plans.

i resigned to the spin maker's ambitions. if you know this music,
you know damned well you have very few options. move! or be moved—
either path runs through Paradise—eventually. move! or suffer the
consequence. the DJ just hammered in Louie Vega's version of "Dance"
by 3 Winans Brothers featuring The Clark Sisters, like a clarion call to
Friday evening prayer. the unction lends a carpenter's encouragement to
the small of my back,

> oh! look at me when I should be cryin' /
> u make me wanna DANCE!

Afro Mosaic Soul is a litigious tribe of serious house-music dancers; crew don't always take kindly to the newbies who may not yet fully understand the language on the floor. movement is the only justice these dancers sanction! dancers are the club's beast of burden—each mule totes their own weight. burdens bury inside the rhythm, regardless one's private mood.

each dancer's sacrifice floods the room and propagates a collective force with its own vexing frequency. all night this wireless cord taunts the DJ's fickle pulse, incites the DJ's nimble hands to heed the Spirits in the room. this underground dance floor imbibes conversation across Dimensions! the needle on that Kim English and Frankie Feliciano groove sings

> *I can't believe that you are gone, but I'm missin' you.*

the lyrics crush me back in time—make me believe i am eleven years old again and i just found out my mommy died. in the baseline i hear the footsteps first. i remember the patent leather patter of those faceless beings who came to tell me Mommy passed away where I cannot reach her—ever?

> *I tremble when I hear your name /*
> *There ain't nothing to ease the pain /*
> *The thought of being without you I just can't face.*

my knees buckle inside a wail discovering its own way station in my throat. i have already lost track of where i laid my things. i grieve myself into a crouch absent of solace. i move.

> *Oh, never thought I could feel like this /*
> *How I long for another kiss /*
> *I'd do anything just to feel your warm embrace.*

a whole bowel of sorrow—undigested still—hurls from my spleen,
then flatlines into a moan. my entire body rolls because the DJ, the snare,
and that got-damned piano, have launched a quickening knee, high up
onto the top side of my spine between the shoulder blades. resistance is
meaningless in the unfettered company of lyric and grief and sound.

my entire body has morphed into a Ouija board planchette;
somehow it knows if i ever want to be close to Mommy again, i must
echolocate to the frame of that stack speaker now and hold on to it. this
close, the subwoofer holds my mourning in abeyance and rubs it raw.
alive suddenly aches like a death i cannot describe. and the grief—the
damned grief—moves, curls itself into a fist. on its wet way down to my
waist, my lower back and hip liberate a movement in space i did not know
i owned. this full-bodied elegy—accompanied now by Gil Scott-Heron's
"The Bottle" and Blaze's "Sapporo"—is a prayer for her. a prayer only
she will understand, and i feel Mom's gentle palm, as real as any yesterday
i've ever known, rest invisibly flat against my navel.

> *"boy, come, press your finger here with me*
> *against your belly,"* she whispers. *"i am*
> *your mother"*

as if i don't know her voice.

> *"tonight i come, because even in Heaven, i*
> *have not yet found the grace to ask my son*
> *for permission"*

my hand in hers on my belly is a fistula of hot ice.

"grief too is a blessing,"

I hear her say,

"if you make it move."

i moved then and i have never stopped. this underground movement
is immune to time and booths and crates and stubborn DJs who refuse
to understand they have a ministry—and not a career—on their hands.
bona fide dancers know we have a power too—a talk-back slingshot in
our dance that will strike DJs dead if they dare to defy the Spirits in those
damned sadomasochistic black-and-gray plastic crates.

FOR MARJORY

A Tribute

Sexy—the way a river make music. A den recesses inside a shaman's drum. Each House party, a choir practice. She had New York City Underground tethered to the Afro-punk quilt in the grout beneath her tongue. She slayed us there, astride a carousel of vinyl and waist.

Lovers and apostles hold fast a congregation slung to her lanky suede pew. She danced a women's dialect. Ballet betrothed to majesty and grace. Thunder-light drench in Her Reign. Inculcated, dance is a spirit's disciple! Make the body free! Our joys fold round grief unspoken. Our

desire tucked away somewhere safe, someplace warm. Lips roasted Yoruba & peanut unlatch the kissing gates to her ivory-coveted smile.

baby powder / and thump-thump-thump / oceans rite / brooms jump / freestyle / free spirit / and fresh pumped blood / high knees / arms /

windmill salve of smooth warm thigh / street style / shaken / stirred / skin salt and jasmine / head wrapped / in sandalwood and grape-seed oil.

Sweat, an altar for all us enchanted by holy ghosts. She lent our Underground a parachute of a rich-tented cotton sheet. A giant peace

of Ten City
Heaven, Heaven, Heaven.

SWAG ON FLEEK

World Is a Ghetto
(Rehearsal Version)

"Beetles in the Bog"

brisk like any animate
form of resistance

"War is Coming"

the way he walk
leak his coordinates—

baseball cap tell you
what music he listen to

"Where Was You At"

may not tell you
where he from

"City, Country, City"

brim sloped to shadow the scent
of his saltwater trail

"The Cisco Kid"

his nose a divining compass
through cannabis slopes

& hip-hop mountains where water always mean
the promise of snow

every block is a slalom
an avalanche breaks uphill

eyes lash and bridle
a thorny disposition

He walks like an ambition   **"58 Blues"**
in a   **"Four Cornered Room"**

because nothing in him stands still—

not his lust nor his dreams
nor his grief nor his hope

He ooze like   **"Freight Train Jam"**

don't you know it's true
that for me and for you

                                   "The World Is A Ghetto"

of progeny and sweat hung between
headphones and fresh-worn thighs.

OPEN CYPHER

After Craig muMs Grant

     Hell naw, this ain't no church
    But the poets is here. Come to worship
     in his name

    Come by here
    Sweet muMs,
    Come by here

Welcome to the ole-time meetin' ground,
where the poet, the roach, & the parishioner
swarm in cosplay. Antennae & raised hands

make the room wave for a great man.
A juke joint and Rhodes organ sucks
wind on a talk-shit corner. Knock-knock

earring chimes, wash over the Bronx River Jordan.
And the music make. Like niggas ain't never
had nobody but themselves,

they buildin' | they boro
they street-cred | they set
they peeps | they crew.

Here ain't quite like the Oz we remember,
but its sure as hell damn close. Poets know how
to clear out a room; let the people back in

Open the cypher, now close it
Open the cypher, now close it

Come by here Sweet muMs,

We are all here to see you.
Da Bronx lent its rock &
cradle to all of Us

—the Irish, the Dutch, the First
Nation. The German, the Italian, the Eastern
European. Puerto Rico, Haiti, Kingston, New
Guinea, & the Great Migration—

when those rare earths rose to
press that Sugar Hill sound. Rezone
our tenement trespass into nano-futures

fit for the global & the subversive.
Tonite we come as a project housing
a universe of need.

Love, word, bars, sage,
crushed grief, mock the origami
cranes tempting our belief.

Bullying them even to puff open
—breathe new life into this broken beat
bleating into a groove.

Heads nod in unison, synchronized to
the line formation of an NoI i-Robot parade.
Shoulders hunch, right foot fall forward.

Drum fall out the larynx of a sample Orisha sky
Niggas rock, Oz shakes. The world shakes!
The lot of us never stop shaking

> *Hell naw, this ain't no church*
> *But the poets is here. Come to worship*
> *in his name*

> *Come by here*
> *Sweet muMs,*
> *Come by here*

Shell top | acid-wash | fronteras
gun run | product push | bomberos
suede down | hustle | double Dutch,

hopscotch | boost. | Purple tongues,
grape Now and Laters | top shelf, Monster
juice. | Lucy loose at the bodega

with its wartime provisions.

Hands up! | Don't shoot! | The gristle,
the crunk | the grind | the whistle.

And still he occupied those emcee bones

Nigga knew a pen had to be a metaphor
for the gods in you. The OGs in cypher,
the emcees on deck. The spit out yo' neck,

The blood spilt and split.
Between two hills; the four
wall block nurse a city of dreams

> *niggas choose,*
> *niggas is chosen*
> *which one is you?*

Everything we do here is me & you

> wrong | light
> dark | right | pop rock
> lock | fight | flight

Everything we do here is me & you

> *niggas choose,*
> *niggas is chosen*
> *which one is you?*

———————

    muMs

Rest, King—Rest

E.T.

Close Encounters with Nina Sim.one

nina sim.one in her own words b the proof we was visited
by aliens. entered the stratosphere @ the Village Gate.

> *Her name is Peaches / Her parents were slaves.*

Witness! the cosmic microwave background at the back of
her throat. a contralto transceiver, spites space, bites time.
black-box transpond, guttural somber death rattle. Holy
Ghost gravel fine-ground into Warwick's coffee and cream.

> *One Day I woke up and I cld fly /*
> *Be ye transformed by the renewing of your mind.*

How can you be a star? and not reflect the times? see-line
woman faces off Mrtn Luthr King. el niña Nephilim strap
wingspan on an Old Testament eye for an eye. her dispatch
is not non-violent. righteous Revolutions hook left, face

down *West*. prostrate east toward
Stokely, Hansberry, Garvey, Malcolm.

genius broadcast pitched perfect; traipse the earth's bipolar.
her Delta, mercurial as it is magnetic. her fields is cotton
piano and aurora—leave Mr. Backlash with da Blues. metro-
nome resonate ultraviolet divine Feminine make Nina's

aesthetic a hologram of classical black.

Absolut

|Black|

has
a Spectrum. black wrath black gold, kundalini, transgender.
she. teleported into a den of smug ideas and elegant people.

drove them all insane. They! won't never know the vertigo-
crucifix worn by a name one does not Own.
Where you come from Nina? I comes from a
chemical imbalance! I am Nefertiti's
alchemical Reincarnation.

My skin is black / my arms are long / my hair is like wool /
My skin is yellow / my hair is straight and long.

My hallucinations thought I should be the same color all over.
On the laser beam with my husband, Andy. the man who tied
me up and raped me—he was also my nephew. each scream
too human to be heard. in a world few people understand

I am what I am / Don't belong here don't belong there /
Sometimes at night / The walls talk back to me /
They seem to say / Wasn't yesterday a better day.

"I seen God in Africa having as little to do with human beings
as possible and in some weird way, I'm at peace."

see-line Woman dressed in green.

Anunnaki wear silk stockings with golden seams. Interstellar
Orisha make my mission impossible: Go make the people
curious Nina 'bout where they come from. Go make the
people curious Nina 'bout where they come from. They come......
....
..............from the beginning!

BARCLAYS CENTER

The Day Before the Day After Tomorrow

new moon

What a honey moon
Bang Zoom straight to the moon, Alice—to the Moon!
The Nets at Barclays a lesson learned
Jay-Z's borough cannot be owned.

Brooklyn brewed thick-lipped and bold:
Barbra Streisand, Jackie Robinson, Shawn Carter,
Christopher Wallace.

Fulton Street & Eastern Parkway's treasure map,
a tributary, ambled through a borough:
shorn and un-crumbled by eminent domain;

a quarry of fans fused over Dodgers' heartbreak
at Ebbets Field and an end of summer 1991 race riot
between the Blacks & the Jews.

A park at Prospect shoulders Flatbush Avenue's thick neck.
A museum, a botanical garden, a library after Labor Day's
Caribbean parade, a Grand Army Plaza of monuments
and gazebos nurse the diaspora in their marble stone

and weathered brass lap. A turn north runs you to the scalp
of the Manhattan Bridge and a sea of change barely holds on
to histories come & gone, lives and loves lost & found.

waxing crescent

1995, under cover of day we landed
at an Atlantic corner circa 4th Avenue.
A requiem harbor sat at the northeast outpost
to Spike Lee's 40 Acres and A Mule

I remember

Frank's Lounge | Cecil Taylor | Erykah Badu
Sunday Tea Party | Mos Def | jessica Care moore
Saul Williams | Sarah Jones | Brooklyn Moon Cafe

I remember

Talib Kweli | Carmen Renee | Tish Benson | Universes |
Wood Harris | Francks Deceus | Liza Jesse Peterson | Shelley Nicole
Latasha Natasha Diggs | Sha-Key | muMs the Schemer

Imani Uzuri | Marcia Jones | Carl Hancock Rux
Jasiri | pierre bennu | Kymbali | Suheir Hammad
Juakali | mTkalla | Sol | Rha Goddess | Staceyann Chin

first quarter

1996, Erykah—me, my words her throat, a drum—
onstage at Nuyorican Poets Cafe.

Her living room hung atop a Moshood storefront
at Fulton Street & South Portland.

The brown-baked early afternoon
Fort Greene sun oiling her parquet floor.

The tow of incense & hair wrapped tall
dreams piled high.

I remember those eyes.

> *rehearsals rehearse themselves don't they?*

> *waxing gibbous*

1998, Mos popped up at my house party
452 Washington Avenue between Park Place & Classon.

2001, One 1 o'clock afternoon
long after Black Star had shot to the moon

on Bergen Street just off Flatbush,
a blowgun shot away from the old Nkiru Books
where Talib used to clerk and help run
Mrs. Miller's black-owned bookstore—

Talib called my name from across the street.
I crossed we smiled whole-bodied.

My heart jumped up in my chest.
Not because Talib called my name.
Because I heard sprung from his larynx
the blitzkrieg history of how he knew—

How we knew—

my name and sundry others was worthy of being called:

[insert your name here]

full moon

Names: [insert yours here]
Names: [insert yours here]

Names canopy this Kings County
Agnominal rainforest; born decades before
dead-letter hashtags try on for size

to necklace the remembered and the forgotten
conceived inside a virtual terroir.

Names: [insert yours here]
Names: [insert yours here]

Names come and came, danced and drenched,
Names spun and sang and prayed,

Names kissed and brushed and loved and
laughed and leaned and learned

Names wrote, painted and praised, and
offered up with joy their instruments

in the feeding of our collected sky:

waning gibbous

We the living & the dead.
The well-lived & the passed-on
will all find our way to the Mother Ship
—that Barclays sand—
by way of its dark matter

Underground.

They will call it The Reconvening
All 19,000 seats of Noah's ark
constructed atop the old train yard

xo skeleton splayed in the palate of our ancestors.
Still—our brownstone rust rinses the rain.

Afro-roots ride or die.
Their proceed will outpace

these hipster high-rises
in this new mammon town

remember
?

third quarter

They built the city on top us
Never knew we were here
Until scuttle bone would give up its marrow

Pep (Frantz Simpson) my friend
one of the greatest visual artists
ever not known.

Were as if this world in real time Refused
to learn his Name

Pep

5' 6" maybe 5' 7" a light skinned Haitian American
elfin-slave to inspiration

& magic.

Betrothed to believing
art & brotherhood

—the kind you die for—

is all there ever was.

Sometime one headstone
might as well be an exponent.

Pep lived & created at 560 State Street
in the felt shadow of the old train yard
in a hangar-walled duplex.

Home, Pep made his way
his genius a reflex already.

He reconfigured a new manhood
contravent to circumstance
contravent to the wind.

Wry smile. Squinted eyes squared north
And transfixed to that vaulted ceiling.

A brewery of blunt-lit red lips
kissed the bodies and bodies of work
used to dress those walls.

All that color and dark and light
hung high on Heineken and promise

remember?

the artist formerly known.

>   *A stranger. A handyman*
>   *for this Underground*

The promenade of women auditioning to be his muse.
Most I remember by their giggles and by the way each
had taken their shoes off by the front door.

Men inherit no language for loss.
It's been years. Getting over it!
never quite prevails as an option.

Pep was

A laugh hoisted to a wingspan that did cause us
to believe—as much as we could feel—
we were men made ready to take over the world.

waning crescent

Genius & fame do not ship the same.
Sometimes one begets the other.

Sometimes they kiss

and crush each other into pieces.
Most times they simply glide past unrequited

if only to flirt and wave like happy gales in the night
on their way home to who knows where.

Remember Pep
Remember Zook too—

Craig Davis was a master of ceremonies
if there ever was one.

Brothers, consummate artists, friends gone too soon.

Zook's going-home service December 19, 2013
Lawrence H. Woodward Funeral Home
1 Troy Avenue & Fulton Street,

Ntozake our Queen
[with whom Zook was collaborating at the time of his death]

rolled in by her longtime assistant on her wheelchair throne

come to pay her self homage.
Say her goodbye to one of our Kings.

I wept then
I weep now.

Some phrases form rainbows before they are words

Pep   •   Zook   •   Bang   •   Zoom

To the moon, Alice
To the Moon!

Each phase | A moment
          Each moment | A breath

inside a name
[insert yours here]

Black holes win in the end
Brooklyn will reconvene its Universe of stars.

new moon

name [insert yours here].

MANHOOD:
A BOY'S
CALCULUS

CALCULUS I, II, III

man hooded masquerade
a museum erected out of papier-mâché stone,
blue cotton-candied walls hung thick and long
with rooms full of master's Egos

copied Cats
cut and paste
plantation's hegemony
onto trace paper canvas

young guns born too brown for they britches
pen in to kindergarten's cage
where boys are convinced, this calculus

—how one body
relates to another—

that disturbs all the peace

is the same as learning
their one two threes

evidence contrary to belief
our boys learn fast
science must be, I guess?

a hypermasculine story
washed brains don't rinse so simple
in and out of class
the curriculum writes itself

soft boys die hard
hothead & class clown grow contagious;
broad shoulders & differential equations
caliber inches into Glocks

every where we look
Our highest dimensions
Learn their limits
Without degrees

KANYECHUKWUEKELE

"Let's Give God Praise"

1.

Dude blink! Glory gone black just that
quick. Right story wrong place-time, right?

Boys on the block call me Platinum
and I'm ok with that. I'm okay with that.

I am a stolen good. Platinum is God's creation
and not one of my mundane accomplishments.

I do not know who Kanye is, and
neither does he—perchance not yet.

mind I lost momma, way past the sky.

Kanyechukwuekele
(Let's give God praise)

Walk Jesus! Fly ride!

God don't need to copyright his own material.
Context is everything. First introduction to
an American Express was a one-way cruise
through the Atlantic—took 6 to 8 weeks;

meanwhile merchants out of
Liverpool, Bristol, and London

synonym bonds and chattel to blood-let
the endless veins of Imperial credit.

Shorty! White short errrbody save hisself

the Bank, the Bank, the Bank is the Advent
of white-man divination. Casper,

like Barclays, mere an Oracle.
whose first order of business

is that ghastly ecumenical invocation
for Us to: leave our good faith at Home.

2.

Chukwu, Chineke, Chi, Ala

Niger Delta, alluvial and Igbo, noble and
element, deposit the petrol wealth of Creation

into the banks of the Brass River. Black gold stockpile
soon-gone-a-Jamaica, Barbados, Haiti, Virginia, and Platinum.

> *Slave shift, no sick days this ain't no pick up*
> *work. ship wrecks what it takes. Shorty still*
> *ain't shit, they called next on space.*

3.

Is it how we sell records?
Is it how we break them?

> *Hits write, right? But is the mind right? mines*
> *writes rhymes and pressured speech right, right*
> *right.*

Is it how we resist oxidation
in dank moist air?

> *I count! The other people count?*
> *Maybe. Do not count on me unless you*
> *wish to be forsaken*

> *Maafa, Maafa*

> *no thing fair goes there*

Is it how we bun sugar and gin
Southern comfort out of fresh-pick cotton?

Is it how we baffle corrosion
—even at high temperature?

      Peace nyah stay dere, nyah stay dere.

     Maafa, Maafa

Is it how we insure the dawn
of capital in Lloyd's London

or how we corpuscle the American
Corporation?

     —JPMorgan Chase, Brown Brothers
     Harriman, New York Life, FleetBoston,
     Aetna, AIG, Brooks Brothers, Norfolk Southern,
     Wells Fargo, Wachovia, Bank of America—

How else do brown bodies, lost at sea,
sinter into credit-bearing instruments?

     Trust believe all my records keep.

Context is Everything

so what? I ain't sign shit.

American Express
had no dress code—no dress code at all.

4.

Platinum is Chukwu's creation,
and not one of my mundane accomplishments.

> *Holy choir! I admit it! Man its the numbers!*
> *The staged pop-ups, the fake hollers, puffed*
> *jackets, black hoods, high rollers, quick*
> *traffic and goads of internet trash.*

I do not know who Kanye is,
and neither does he.

> *tek mine. Blaow blaow blow all 9 lives. Who know*
> *who Kanye West is? Ye may be AI. How many*
> *records mill out that basement? graves shift. still*
> *ain't made shit but mania and flowers. Damn, when*
> *did the chatbots learn how to spell blaow?*

All the figures lay out. By the end of those 6 to 8 weeks,
good faith and credit show signs of attrition.

By spaceship and fly.
By spaceship and fly.

The lot of us, left over, never inured to our tongue
a fondness for the scum now flourished like algae

on the Atlantic pond. We pre-date history
unlike Columbus. 5,500-year-old Platinum ornaments

found sintered off Ecuador's alluvial coasts,
prove trace elements of the ancient's mind

exonerates-not the bubonic erasure of
Precontact Native American intelligence

5.

European metallurgists could not manipulate
Platinum until the 19th century.

Swing down sweet chariot lemme ride

Tomorrow is an opportunity without patent.
God don't need to copyright his own material—

Let the AI ride; it is gon' learn from
us, right? Train it on the merchandise.

Context is everything. Our most Original re-cycle.
Chukwu, Chineke, Chi, Ala.

Maafa, Maafa

in the right light Platinum
humbles all of creation.

Let's give God praise!
Kanyechukwuekele

Walk Jesus! Fly! Look like Ye and
the AI gon' go ride without us, way,
way, way past the sky.

HUGHES ME A RAINBOW—GHAZAL

Colored is: equal parts Sun and equal parts Harlem;
equal parts apparitions shoot-up junk acid rain

between the Hudson and East Rivers a gem-cut page
ripples, American as heartbreak runs in the rain

asexual is not a noun north of Manhattan
ragtime, jazz, bebop, paint the town bright red in the rain

Blues plot the brilliance his larynx refused to imbue
in uptown quarter's paper doors spell poems in the rain

renaissance has a different mouthfeel than the gentry
palate in refurbished sidewalk cafes in the rain

words is a spectrum come out to frolic in the rain
Langston Hughes rainbows before flags flew in the rain

EVERY WHERE ALIEN

i am unabridged; / walk over me at your peril! / Your fix broke free /
i am an infinity imbibing time— / an ancestor's scribe born without
papers / aroused & wet / whose liquidity am i? / i am / absolved of

gender at Orgasm / i engender   billions of beings. / iClouds
are not safe-deposit boxes—   / Google won't have me
found; / no cookies bear   my namesake. / No cookies
bear my namesake. /   Nations stymie with a kiss. An
Empire's progeny /   infuse the pan sauces that
survive / i am the   black, called the kettle / just
to say: i love you   & i think you are hot! /
How high is   Colorado really? / If
they've only
now
pot / is   discovered
of the   the alchemy
Porridge   Gods. /
                                                is not a
                                                medicine—
it   is   simply
good   for you.
/ I   n i is the
                                                Divine prototype
come   up out of   Africa /
             consciousness   is god's multiple
personality disorder / we   Believe belief
belies an   antonym in lived   language / the
absence   of belief   comprises
Death   /   bereaved   of
its
metaphysical
powers. /
/ as in the end   !DeaD!
Metaphor is magic— /   of dying. /
beget quantum   insists Illusions
now—follow me! Eh /   Mechanics / even
the things / i wished i had   never   i have already been all
definition of ambition— /   been; / #this!: the very
Movement! / Sans desire,   to make yourself a
out flaccid thing. / Drama is   time is a stretched-
Desire's Desire matters our   aboriginally human— /
                                    universe. / At our absolute best
/ we are all self-starters / self-inflicted victims of arson / watch us burn!
Baby. / We are flaming Flames / unflappable as the wind— / the wind
is a pusher Man; / top and bottom / are equivalent dimensions / all
equilibriums spell BORING / over and over again. / Yes we are no mad
/ & normal absents our Universe; / thick with desire / replete with the
darkest matter / we are every where alien / except in our own skin.

99

SIZED TO X

x is single

x is fluid

x is changes

Malcolm is paroled to Us.
Elijah's mouthpiece—an expert
marksman. Kill shot: Negro self-image.
That masculine brand, the silk screen to
his pastel frame. Malcolm wears on us so well.
History lies with its own cache of evidence.

x is protean

x is elastic

x is adaptive

x is adroit

x is diversified

Little, cocks that free man's dialect.
Sometimes he rhyme. Sometimes he reason.
Precise tongue blunts a race into its senses.
Coordinates set to lucid & heat seeking.
Gravitas, snark-kissed, evinces introspection.
Each event horizon owns a bottom lip.

x doubles

x squares

x is not capricious

x is not shifty

x is not slippery

Insight must be a form of condensation.
Raindrops keep fallin' on our head.
Nothing seems to fit.

x is not spasmodic

x is not iffy

x is not altered

x is not wavering

Surnames size to X.

x is not yo-yo

x is not temperamental

A cellblock grows a masjid into a country. Mind,
the harvest, reconfigures out of street boot & toe jam.
Wiggle, wiggle it! There's room to think our way
out the gout enshrined in the US Constitution.
Black, yellow, pretty: *Red* got no relatives named
Gandhi or National Mall in the family tree.

x is not uncertain

x is not unstable

x is not plastic

x is not altered

x is not pliable

x is not unsettled

x is not unsteady

x is not facile

x is not vacillating

x is not waffling

x is varied

x is variant

x is variable

x is various

x is variegated

x triples

x is noble

x is masterful

Malcolm's naps
dream not. King, Queen,
Love thy self! Love the Nation!
—Thy Kingdom un-come!—Absolute
faith is always a high-risk investment.
Behind black rimmed glass,
righteousness finally flies
in a biped garrison.

El-Hajj Malik el-Shabazz's laser eyes press
zoom. In this cotton-pickin' land, the pot
was melted in the pot maker's hands.

We are all aliens,

grandfathered into a west Atlantic cult
of snake oil & Pilgrims. Selling an anecdotal
Constitution lathered in tar & Dred Scott.
Rule! No Exceptions! Convert or else!
Devil keep a filthy house in these
former Colonies. Log cabins
float & pimp they stool
pigeon by any means.

Thank you, *Omowale!*
Thank you, *Malcolm!*
The son who has come home.

p.s.
Thank you
Forever.

THE SACRIFICE

How available must one be to hear the mind of God?
  Have her run you a river bath
    right where America's hanging Oaks dangle
      their hiss-screech confession

atop subsoil too blood-black to ever overfarm
  spell-cast instruments withstand atom chatter
    trace the Creole aftermath of collided matter
      the metronome hides the ever-demanding Queen

masturbators die in the swarm
  an orgy agog,
    disciplines pathos and craft into abandon
      —ensures the freest rule

hi-hats govern their private brush with submission
  brass-knuckle acquiescence make way

for tresillos ripened on a blue vine
  comrades towed along with nothing but a phrase

the Jubilee bleeds through fractured characters;
  whole notes tell less than half their story.

Sometimes it hurts too much to speak.

Jazz is the province of a crucible Genius;
   a compulsive's life sentence
      addictions arouse roux—

seize a letting-go that won't stop stroking
   the Cambrian side of orgasm
      mortal hands graze the heart of God

How many Miles must one person travel to rinse?
   In this bitch brew well

How many?

   Miles?

Jazz anchored him well inside the pusher man's fist
   Master cuffed himself to his field hands

Miles required his men make flesh
   the swarm inside his head.

In the rare case he needed a woman,
   to make his music, he loved on her too.
      Co-conspirators All

In the only freedom he ever knew.

Onstage, in the studio, in session,
   Miles laid over his horn a sound so human it chants
      the freed-open pleasure of language and worship.

Ritual sacrifice in service of the sound—Holy
    ragtime hovers over a country of wounds
        to conjure a healing on its own excruciated terms.

Lovers groomed with the gentle push of
    his raspy voice in their ear. His shined horn
        in their soul.

Miles circled.

A tango of high notes dog-whistle
    their uninjured release

Miles's wives unlucky charms.
    The minstrel needs his toys.
        The pimp needs his hoes—

Miles insisted he be the object
    emptied into their Possession.

A showcase of abbreviated stars,
    they light had to travel too far

A procession of fine cars towed
    Those All-American Miles
        rode : those : women : too : hard.

black and white don't leave a man with choices
    King of every hall he ever played.

relinquished his hall pass whenever he left the stage
   through the back door

fans : wives : women : children took up their residence
   in the only half-ass corner they could fit
     crushed on every side

by the otherwise soul-consuming
   weight of the music.

In the Master's house the price
   gruesome to watch him reign.

THEY CROWNED HIM

An Elegy to Kalief Browder

1.

For all Kalief Browder knew, he was born of the Virgin Mary
circa 1993; state wrapped him up in swaddlin' clothes,
delivered him downriver to Momma's two-story brick house
across the street from the Bronx Zoo

Momma nicked his name: Peanut—
tiny, hardly fragile; took to roast on concrete
playgrounds. Asphalt baked slow-brown and
streetwise, flint by the Bronx River sun

Peanut. By age 6,
he was an 8-pack calisthenic,
stood up straight and happy
inside his big brother's shadow

By sophomore year @ New Day Academy,
2010, the year he was took,
Peanut developed signature flavors—
smelled his own salts   in and out of shell

Teachers tell us he was equal parts
sly : smart : and not too studious.

Seem like I—*Peanut said*—left home
one day, went to a party

Nightfall found me and my boy a blues band.
On the road: runnin'. We was arrested
on 186th, May 15th, 2010, four-eight precinct
Bronx County, Belmont section

Charted our regression line through Arthur Avenue
on our way back to da crib: Lights! Camera! ACTION!

da Barrio talent scouts rolled up on us

put us up for audition | made me take off my cap
gave me a new identity | crowned me with too many..

Flash! | body
squandered | evidence
inside assault | and battery

Flip! | Teenager
Youth offender | Upside down
Negative charge | on top:

felony 2nd-degree.

some somebody say I stole
a backpack | a credit card | digital camera,
iPod touch | and 700 dollars.

Little bag a Peanuts sang his self a Blues

Mr. Charlie! Mr. Charlie!
The bars in this song too heavy

My tenor got no business
playin' the bass, Mr. Charlie!
For this Rikers Island band

When can I go home?
When can I go home?

Bronx County Bookies wear navy,
jockey their bets on my survival.
Rode me hard often, like any good game of chance

In these Belmont Stakes

May be he done it | May be not
May be he win it | May be not—

Race don't run without the horses!

Got my offshore account @ Central Booking,
belly buoy-full of knots. Bus, above deck,
cast anchor, over to Riker's;

One nerve I had left wept! Innocent!
Knuckles white as snow

Regardless—New York City Department of Correction
gots they own shows to produce outs yonder
on that Middle East River Gethsemane got 4,000 acres
of production space nestled between boroughs of borrowed time

discovered. | a falling star
writ | a leading role
speaking part | @ children's table

Never heard the one-line avowal
Incarcerated at the back of my throat

I swallowed whole chased Hail Mary
With one everlasting plea:

I am not guilty I am Not guilty I am
Not guilty I Am not Guilty God
Father! All Jehovah's witness
Know I am not!

    2.

Kalief Browder's bail was set @ $10,000.
Momma would not afford that.
Family's only defense had to be the US Constitution;
6th Amendment guarantees a speedy and public trial

Except in the shower @ Robert N. Davoren Complex,
Department of Corrections. Where there are no cameras.
Bronx County Hall of Justice fade to black!

Law's best intentions
wear sackcloth and ash

6th Amendment séance
whisper in ever more furtive voices:

felony case must be brought to trial within 6 months of arraignment
felony case must be brought to trial within 6 months of arraignment

In da Bronx District Attorney's Office, time marks
with driftwood stick etched in Orchard Beach sandstorm

Judge just a Whip
going through the motions

State ain't ready | to try its case
Judge robe | Black magic
wand whipped | space-time
Adjourned | to black hole

until the next court date. Well!
Inside legal limits of Kalief's six months
of struggle, 3 years perished

—built for us a wailing wall in those
1,110 days—

Three whole Memorial Day weekends
made it to they Resurrection;

Each end of May did not never pass
Go. Would not get out of jail free

Hope deferred 31 times below the event horizon
800 *Nights of Solitude*

Get it? | The Law takes
Practice | blood sport and wager

fill the seats | pay all the bills
purchase | Yankee Stadium season tickets

Floodlights | are epic
@ this | Grand
Concourse | Court jester

Bazaar

Gethsemane's Poor, ill-afforded circus
transmogrify into currency.
Every Body else gets paid;

Kalief's public defender earns
$75 an hour at least

to crush Peanut | into an oil
make him slow | and impermeable;
smooth him | like butter

into his trouble | make the charges stick:
Guilty. Plea! | Please! Goddammit
This. Way. | Everyone

goes home happy—eventually.

Only way anyone gets delivered
from this ectopic pregnancy

3.

How do you say *Desaparecidos*?
In a New York Yankee accent

My whole adolescence gutted
All my teenage organs entrails:

friends switch | to zone defense
After a while | I become
Jurassic trip | to the zoo

Basketballs leave | the paint high dry
Video games | asphyxiate in haggard air
pockets stripped | mauled for any all contraband

Fine girls | and black-light parties
Prom night | high school graduation
All: Disappeared! | on my very first trip abroad.

In the Middle of that East River,
Peanut has no easy allies

Repressed canisters of testosterone splay everywhere.
The hormone imbalance rots the air
with a latent gang-bang adolescent spunk
CO tribunals prefer torture to interrogation.

Alas! for boys like Peanut there is no peace in Jerusalem

Boys who believe
Justice is a whole food
And Truth lives in Zion.

They fed him Ramadan in his teenage sanctuary.
God had to tell him: Solitary has no plea for Freedom

Peanut listened.

Buried—like all the other inmates—
his life's achievements inside the white
plastic bucket furnished by the state

This jailhouse safe-deposit box
stayed on his person.   worked for him
overtime doing double-triple duty:

interstitial | talisman
pillow | weapon
accomplice | friend

Otherwise! Peanut denied the state
their right to make him invisible

Corrections Officers, by now, had to have borne witness
to that scant, hopeful stitch woven into Peanut's brow

A shallow mutant flame hung to the base of his throat;
its treble echoed whenever he spoke up on his own behalf

bitter | steel
reinforced | concrete
womb | of Difference

Outcast | with-in-difference
Insist! | Any biblical notion of Justice

be contracted out!

4.

12 foot by 7 foot
Peanut walks the plank

In the Central Punitive Segregation Unit,
human cells show no signs of differentiation

The stasis metastasizes into a need for palliative care.

On the mainland the Judges play God.
State-sponsored motions move like terror

All clocks stop except the one on Peanut's ticking time.
Motion after motion accrue no movement.
Each successive step an immolation

Plank. | Left.
Less | and less
Room. | for error.

A clatter of trouble rattled inside Peanut's head;
his whole heart crumbled into one cell
until he craved nothing but the cross

had to be Nothing! but the Blood for me

Impetuous land of milk and honey
promised the guileless find rest in eternity

Going up Yonder, Innocent!
Will be a longer word than Infinity

    5.

Were you there?
When they crucified my Lord
Were you there?

What if I told you grandiose delusion
is narrative nonfiction in our Universe?

They shoot stars like me!

No body doubles | Graphic novels
grow palate | for animation
all my stunts | are real

magic.

When I told the doctors @ Harlem Hospital's mental health unit:
I am Jesus Christ!
I told them the Truth!

I overthrew the money changers' table
because they peoples was watching me
on my brand new 27" flat-screen TV

I wonder.

If my act be worth they trouble?
Had I trashed an older-model box TV

Did you see? The video
up on *The New Yorker* website

Didn't nobody believe me!
When I was pitchin' my stories

Had no abstract on hand
I took them to da spot

word for word | *blow by blow*
still for still | the money changers

thought my storyboard had
a special flare for the dramatic

Please! Beat! Me! Peanut cried.
Body blows make me feel

the Jesus in my marrow.
He! Helped Me.

Endure the pulp I become
When they look at me

Look! I am bleeding now
from every pore in Gethsemane

What else? | Have I to believe?
Jesus become | my only theory for Being.
Didn't he? | Save the whole world with his story

What if the Resurrection got posted on YouTube
How many more would believe?

Mr. Charlie! Mr. Charlie!
Beat! Me! Until I am blue
just like you

Peanut cried his self to sleep 1,000 times,
hungry with the weight of withheld rations

So many subtractions add up after a while.
Hades wins its trespass to Paradise
down this Villa de la Rosa

Cuffs and hands turn bruise to sorrow
throngs of brown boys, cadres of toy soldiers

come over with they own troubles

Confess! They confess they sins to me!
See the spittle on my face!

Pontius Pilate let them have their way with me.
I became the cross my body could not bear

The help I begged earned me vinegar
for my trouble. Internal bleed be damned

They! would not give me the emergency
dilation and curettage I needed. They!

all just sent me back to my 800-day ectopic pregnancy.

Kalief's blood boiled over 6 times inside Gethsemane.
Strange how infinity manufactures an opt-out option!
Kalief pulled that lever 6 times inside that Riker Island Well

The bedsheet lasso, he fashioned himself
and tied it to the only light he could find

Roped it round his trouble.
Lamb go good with peanuts

Sacrifice is for the living.
Me?

I goes back to my New Day Academy in Heaven.

6.

After 961 days Kalief's 8th judge,
that last wonder of the world,

Judge Patricia M. DiMango
made Peanut her lowest offer:

Plead guilty—she said—to two misdemeanors,
go home right now with time served

My final offer! Only time I swore:
Tell the truth the whole truth so help me God!

Up against 15 years I will make trial my error!
Only plea I have is Heaven and bound

to a calcified will, homesick with trauma.
I will not abdicate the only throne I've been given

Jesus survived because he believed
others could never keep his secrets

I will abstain from false confession!
Nothing else! Let the whole world know

Peanut stayed true

The reliable white plastic bucket
bleeds black wrists

Who? Am I to resist its surgical ambitions

According to Bronx County law,
embryos are not babies

Black, brown teenagers are turtles.
Best they stay in they shell and crack

Put the sharpest edge on my bucket list.
We will slash my wrist

before I gash my tongue,
cross my own conscience

7.

I seen *Peanut* on TV: a 13-minute clip
with Marc Lamont Hill.

New Mister Lawyer Man was on it.
Kalief gon' get his self some money

Saw Peanut's cheeks sit up high; for just a breath,
blush with evidence Peanut was still in there somewhere

Wow! such an easy smile.
Open and light like hearts of
mother-loved boys

Smiles do not always speak of happiness

Lips part | teeth flash.
Confess! | Struggle
tongue | cannot yet twist

into words.

Stowed bruise | sits on
bleeding stool | some pains
do not flush | well behind

closed doors | A Holocaust
is present and | unaccounted for

In between boroughs Kalief stumbled
upon the sins of the whole wide world

Fisticuffs squared off wild inside his head.
He still had to tread water

He tried! God knows he tried!
Balance infarct against percussion

Won't you, Peanut?
Support your wildest ambition

Suicidal ideation con and cuss
the Hollywood hopes of

Rosie O'Donnell and Jay-Z!
H to the izz-O, V to the izz-A

Thank you for trying. Alas!
Even American [CELEBRITY]

is not a panacea.

My end of days is a regression.
Each independent variable depends
on the round-trip back

to Momma's 2-story house on 186th Street

Home. | From school
Home. | From the job
Home. | From meetings with New Yorker reporter
Home. | From class @ Bronx Community College
Home. | From huffpost.com interview

Back home become a room inside my head,
smell of homemade rice and chili,
remembers itself as a trauma

You know how good food smell?
When you can't get any?

State must rest its case. Let me go free

No justice | No trial
No peace | Emptied me
Full | no sense
Heart | entombed
Flailing | at sea

Far from purpose

All that time in Gethsemane for this?

My life. I already knew what that was,
had to think prospectively

I am the Resurrection and the Life!
After I'm gone, they will tell my story

Holy Ghost will not leave you alone!
In Solitary I am the last prophet

to a nation @ #massincarceration
No grave shall hold my body down!

Truth: Here Lies my body
broken for you

Peanut rested his case June 6, 2015.
Lost his soul, cast anchor off AC wire

Momma, tell Mary don't weep.
We finally mades it out Gethsemane

Alive! Jehovah's witness rise!
Salvation cometh, Momma

To all those who dare to believe in Me!

AUTOCORRECT

Dear John, Revelation 1:14–15
After Joel Francois

when you think of black men you do not think of me
it is as if a cotton field blooms a black hole on a twin's heart
a gray, brackish flood thickens into clots
fluidity loses all its water gay bi trans pixel over
into burlap rations kissed tongue swallows
a blackened church autocorrects a middle passage
the taste of god in our throat
in that field where we bent so well
no memory of us folded at the neck
dust settles to ash an urn of afterthoughts
inside black-&-white photographs omissions fill up with rainbows
shadows grow tender to touch ain't a black man
my namesake too? on this threshing floor
oh, how we bowed oh, how we did not tare
hot and sun-oiled through and through
exhausted not the finding of you in our private place
passion tends to its own vices we rehearsed our coal-hot mime
hardwood infused a burning bush builds a special kind of chapel
in these slave quarters lovers pass for kin
a love story records unwritten
unspeakable play labors of love
burning, we would not come down from our cross
on a sunday morning they dared not see

where they dared not look   on a saturday night
congregations worship as men   if only this passover
saved from sin as the ark of the lord come in   the city that never sleeps
half-slave, half-free   brothers rock feigning sleep
stood up in heaven   way jesus loved john
we loved in that field   manumissioned
dressed the dandy out of a burial ground   a misgendered groove on a blues
moaned us a second coming   of the son of man
hair like wool eyes like Gomorrah   bronzed in a glowing furnace
secrets   the throb of rushing waters
floods. a lover's mercy   our only baptism.

JOURNEY:
A SHAMAN'S
NARCOTIC

AUTOCORRECT

The Ayahuasca Remix
Dear Cain, An Open Letter from Gilgamesh & Enkidu

Dear Cain,   "Let us go out [again] to the field"
Abel we could have saved   "I don't know . . .

. . . am I my brother's keeper"   men?
you do not think of us   misfit grunge

queered   commoners and Kings
on the cusp of a city   misogyny

Growing a canyon self-righteous   grander than sin
gorge fill up with sanctimony   the entitled crowd

As if the *civilized* have autocorrected   the beam in their eye
The moat in their sky   a raft of radioactive plastic

in the warming tide   Imagine US, more animal than you?
Cain, Look at me   Enkidu, rabid wild queer

"he was yearning for one to know his heart   a friend"
born raw as source material: Eve water Goddess clay

wild mold   well

Kings ruin quicker than sand   Abel know Eden
less zip code, more ecology   more a state of mind

Cain, The King and I we could have told you
All brothers we are worthy of being saved

the dirtiest ones the horniest ones
Can save a King from their Kingdom can nurse a soul into a civilization

that field had so much promise so much brotherhood in its bones
soil too fertile for that dark a heart if you just would have let it be

Fuck you, Cain way you fucked Abel
in that field absent breath, redacted scripture

crucified US.

AUDEN'S FIRST TWEET ON POLICE BRUTALITY

There Will Be No Peace
A Cento Poem

Let aeroplanes circle moaning overhead
Let the traffic policeman wear black cotton gloves
The darkness blotting out hope, the gale
Prophesying your downfall

There Will Be No Peace

Truculent in pink
Aspect an indulgent blue
What have you done to them?

Nothing? Nothing is not an answer

There Will Be No Peace

Stop all the clocks, cut off the telephone
Bring out the coffin, let the mourners come
In the burrow of the Nightmare

The transatlantic boats
The divination of water
I've found the subject mentioned
In accounts of suicide
"O, show us

History

the operator, the Organiser, Time
the refreshing river."

There Will Be No Peace

Because it dissolves in water
On that arid square, that fragment nipped off from hot
Africa, soldered so crudely to inventive Europe
Through the unjust lands, through the night, through the alpine tunnel

They floated over the oceans

This land is not the sweet home that it looks

There Will Be No Peace

Their eyes have never looked into infinite space
Through the latticework of a nomad's comb
Rivers wait to be tamed and slaves to construct you a tomb

Flashbacks falsify the Past; they forget
The remembering Present
And its colors come back,

The storm has changed you

Beings of unknown number and gender
Unable to tell

A hush before storms
From one after massacres

There Will Be No Peace

A million yes, a million boots in line,
Without expression, waiting for a sign

That carries weight and always weighs the same

There Will Be No Peace

MATRIX

when that all-American divide go digital black and white recode
as zeroes and ones. the colored un-collar themselves. basic
training cotton field, erase the bodies contrived beneath these
stars. stripes keloid into cushions. out-of-body experience ripens
premonition into a muscle.

movers\growers\shakers\food healers\potion makers.
culture holders\field theorists\medicine men\agrarians.
ancestors\gatekeepers\cultural anthropologists.

SEE THRU USER INTERFACE

novel\protest\essay\data nuts\idea tinkers\organic intellectuals.

SEE THRU USER INTERFACE

chemists\mystics\evolutionary psychology\microbiology
master theorists\epistemologists\experimental physicists

SEE THRU USER INTERFACE

dream makers\prodigies\particle colliders\math savants
neural networks\assembly theory\history\information theory
historians\deep learning\neuroscientists.

SEE THRU USER INTERFACE

chatbots\nanobots\cognitive behavioral sciences
field theory\robotics\Rihanna\artificial intelligence,

master composers\session player\script writers\dramaturgy
playwrights.\sculptors\film\cinematography\directors\jazz
giants\master thespians.\supermodels\MCs\rock stars\comics

SEE THRU USER INTERFACE

quilters\painters\animators\storytellers\collagists.\revolutionaries
content creators\master teachers\street corner prophets\the peace people
the strongmen\the narcissists\the schizotypal

SEE THRU USER INTERFACE

Disruptors\agitators\political organizers\gamers\coders
hackers\gamblers. \DJs\street dancers\life coaches\style mavens.
faith healers\master healers\mind tamers\psychoanalysts.

love addicts\psychopharmaceuticals\spirit guides\crypto barons
sex workers\futurists.\clusters A\clusters C\clusters B.\intercessors
interlocutors\Blues singers\spirit workers.

Master practitioners of the common and the uncommon sense.

SEE THRU USER INTERFACE

Negroes been went quantum. dodge all the
silent dashes after the N-word. among the root crops sown to sustain
America's killing fields, pesticides are indiscriminate institutions.

Every self, in this molecular battleground, grows a spirit sense
out of an immune response. a body, a mind, a personality
abstracts a soul into the Amplituhedron:

AfroFutures winnow the magnets out of a brutalized core;
paints the human being into the faint outline
of a more fundamental category.

breath / urge / impulse / pulse / play / rest / test / resist
archive / release / retain / incant / retrain / temper / tamper
erupt / rehearse / invent / decant / do over / drift off
refocus / daydream / reinvent

THE SELF: THE FIRST, THE LAST EXPERIMENT

The memory drill-bit. The solder paste
The caretaker for the epic tools amygdalae
forage out of existence.

SEE THRU USER INTERFACE

THE POETRY OF AMERICA

Amiri Baraka Born Again Inside a 1943 Dali Painting
Salvador Dali, 1943, oil on canvas

the Poetry of America nurse George Floyd's
higher self into its freed ambition.

overwrites the dead text, the dissociated knee,
the acid reflux, the incorrigible chorus,

the baler-crushed box face down
in the asphalt plot, on a too black street.

Momma come too
the wild bloom protest.

      Game time, Ham bone, Hot wing, podcast,
      popcorn, police state, tailgate, Jive turkey

         tweet tweet tweet

      Elon Musk and Peter Thiel, Space X,
      space junk, banana peel

         All the billionaires do is scrape, scrape and whittle,
         whittle away at the indigenous clay.

ever in flux. this desert used to be a plantation
b4 it transitioned into a dust bowl.

ever the same. Native sprawl.
Black cotton. former slave owners invent

a National Football League. male privilege, wifebeaters,
loose-lip canons. NFL draft and brown sugar

sign on the spotted line. knees crouch
in a florid field. crowd consume every down.

Coca-Cola, halftime,
clear bottle, old wineskin

they can't help it. they have to police.
even the touchdowns:

>   *Game time, Ham bone, Hot wing, podcast,*
>   *popcorn, police state, tailgate, Jive turkey*

>   *tweet tweet tweet*

>   *Elon Musk and Peter Thiel, Space X,*
>   *space junk, banana peel*

>   *All the billionaires do is scrape, scrape and whittle,*
>   *whittle away at the indigenous clay.*

Earth too hot for the water.
storm too strong for the living

MAGA hinterland
piss on everything green

climate drip, drip, drip

H-2A visas pimp-walk through human traffic,
wage theft, Starbucks, right-to-work laws,

and good, strong coffee. China on TikTok.
TikTok. rafts split into the crypto current.

Africa markets its mercenary sale.
Republicans so into Russia now.

gender nazis, gun lobby, prehistory
school board, abandon the fresh child blood

under deserted desks
in the campus kill zone

Jesus is a cash crop and a killing field.
Uncle Thomas turns his back

on all the uterus in America. books burn,
ballots vanish from the town square.

Black history reincarnates into smoke.
Kanye and Candace, who put the dull knife in?

Proud Boys pull out the antisemitism
resurrect the Charlottesville Klan.

Game time, Ham bone, Hot wing, podcast,
popcorn, police state, tailgate, Jive turkey

tweet tweet tweet

Elon Musk and Peter Thiel, Space X,
space junk, banana peel

All the billionaires do is scrape, scrape and whittle,
whittle away at the indigenous clay.

Get your box seats and gamble on Reservations
while White supremacy sits on top of Goodell's ass!

referees cry foul in black-and-white uniforms.
these outfits uniforms? or flashbacks?

ain't being born the point of being woke?
or is we all color-blind, biracial, and born again

at 3rd and goal
on Monday nights?

who's marking Time at Washington's monument?
we always spelt Malcolm with an X

Amiri Baraka and LeRoi Jones
Belong to this American Anthology

poems don't die in America, and
neither do their secrets

letters go to the Smithsonian,
brains go to science.

we all die playing America's favorite
pastime or simply from watching the game.

TIME TRAVEL

A Shaman's Journey on Behalf of All the Hashtags
Before and After Eric Garner & Michael Brown

1.

Commodities Trade is not an emerging market

SALT | SPICE | SLAVE

    Everything soil-born prices to dirt.

entrance | wide round | no exit. | hot!

as Mississippi cooked hard in a heat wave.

before CAPITAL
have
Sense | Spirit | Soul | Sanctity

SALVATION.

Atlantic Slave Trade began in the 15th century—

alls we eyes | down here | still tryna decipher

how dark can matter be

Incarcerated?
sentenced to time without light
space now the interminable collapse

Each man bestowed a unique perspective on sorrow
Owns discrete distance from Tomorrow

We might as well start with the Here and Now.
urine and feces curtain down here.

No rooms left for tears or sweat
Shit permeates.

    #periodt!

Nostrils acquire more awareness
than each the senses combined;

Listening | one-way to catch one's breath
Ears insist | best pupils discover blindness

Eyes have no bridge ta lend
menses | smegma | vomit

diarrhea | difficile | morning wood | crust eye
wet dream | new hair | sprout new breast

born at sea | sight absent of Sun
bequeaths its powers to hands

Feel! how Time makes its moves;
Make your own music.

2.

Hearts are beaten down here. | Rhythms Falter.
Hope faint | fade to false | dissolve with sea salt.

the Universe done left Us | a baseline
Asked of us | —in this ship of mezzanines—

Lay your whole body over this soundtrack

Niggahs Is a requiem;
Let the redeemed say So!

through those floorboards   Niggahs was always listenin'
heard how white-man voice   grow warm wings

when they mommas called.   did not yet know none a they words

but all Niggahs know the language
boys speak to they mommas

out of sight near out of mind
invisible bodies queer when they touch
untouched bodies revert to Spirit

Couriers sunburn & Uber
rites hold constant the listing antecedent

remembering makes its own refusal
to learn how to forget

3.

Time dids not mean us well   we had to break it!

stretch vertebrae | flat | creak | threaten to snap.
Where did compact discs comes from?

stank blind gorgeous Niggahs | mades it up
back then | down there | with so much time up against our backs

embezzled breaths siphon
against board, against cage

solitary confinement ruptures into a sea of moans

Eyes shut blink wide-wide open
sea blue-blue black

Hard-pressed | Hard up | locked-in
the unbridled heard them Blues first

God know motherless chile die quick

Grief unrequited shrieks!
Labor induced on that Mother ship.

Waters Wade | nurseries had to rhyme
well before-before | us knew of book or Bible

niggard eyes weren't permissioned to read no way
Damned! Niggahs discovered print in the brand on our backs.

Word made Flesh! Holy Ghosts lay slain all over us.

We lived! with our ancestors
Our ancestors died with us

met Jesus | Oshun
Muhammad | Yemaya

one thousand times each times seven—

cared not verify | what color
what sex | which orientations wes all was

in that pitch   pitch-Black   down under

skin boils   skin peels.

The Gods merely implored us: Leave the choosing to us!

4.

The Explorers, they Fly South for Winter

Caught an Equator
Snatch up all its treasure
Snatched up alls our choices

Options stomped
to the oak sawmill floor
of cotton ball pockets

bruise with the warden's keys

hard-core Niggahs count our own time
add the jingles to our score

Learned Black man's religion
finds its faith in tight spaces

Learned we let Orishas choose
who was gon' live to sing us these, our bitter songs

This what happen when the hyenas pack
Each litter of coal-black puppies

Wall Street bundle its Colored capital
among 747 FedEx next-day air cargo

Niggahs tune in.
Time become a frequency

Told us things Man of Blue-Eye Sea
had as not yet invented.

Confessed: history is a long, stretched-out thing.

Ain't nothin' begun in: 1492   1776   1968

White people's time is all made-up

Who? know where they numbers from.
They never make an available Data Set

We wasn't never the top number
in that 3/5 fifth of Kentucky's bourbon

it was each of our Mothers, for all we knew
the Holy Ghost had now yet chosen
to Passover into that sweet-sweet hereafter

Our Ancestors carried the weight of Paradise
heavy atop their diaphragms.

TIME never forgets how bloodlines collapse,
rafts rig, railroad run Under

Meanwhile | Amazon Prime | @ Lloyd's of London
bodyguard they all too precious Capital

make they preparations   for   the next trip
and the next   and   the next . . .

Niggahs will have thousands of lives.

    5.

When TIME breaks   her pent-up;
she pronounces her piece of America's Pie:

"THOSE Mutha Fuckas! up THERE.
Theys ain't never finna stop bum-rushing you like dogs.
Theys never intends ta finish laying you out lengthwise
in the middle of they asphalt street.

As IF!

Nigghas 'spose ta always just blend
back into they Middle Passage.

As IF!

Alls our livin' ain't got no Spirit.

As IF!   Stevie won't ever Wonder.

     As

If! It ever mattered which faith they professed;
they Catholic visions ain't never offer no confession!"

6.

Blind faith makes a stern Mary;
"Don't Weep!" prenatal choir.

Invisibility ain't what
Wonder Woman make it out to be.

That brier-filled cloak is a painful-painful thing.

Bewildered at first;
could not figure how

—with all that light up there—
a die-cast genome remained so unseen?

Theyz never did see our spirit;
looked right through us

like we was cows and sheep caring their babies.
like we was all One Dark Matter exhibition

curated for the Smithsonian. Niggers the original
cotton gin. Their patent papers prove it

7.

Negro lives on the bright side of Epiphany
Let it rain down on us like hellfire and cop bullets

Our ancestors taught us
simple-simple things:

Take Spirit to see Spirit.

Beneath this Good Ship
They bury their's

—leave it to fall 10,000 leagues under the sea.
Pack black dog in ship; Call it ferry business.

Bark! Project! Bark! Project levels of bull's shit!
Well past the limits of God's creation.

Dead Spirit won't see. Denied Spirit grown
numb. We beat the wild bounce drum

Took us a minute. Niggahs figured it out
—Had to!   New World mathematics

was figuring us out of our minds!

    8.

Won't cease till we finds the way
back to P-town FUNK

when the ship lists heavy and hard
the body fluid pool life & death

Take a sample
Break the beat

same way you broke TIME
Put them in your music

Add them to the score. The whole wide world
will never stop listening

hip-hop pandemic | contagious
chronic disease | of the joints

Patient Zero | isolate
just off Sugar Hill.

Race against time | Infection done gone crossed
the Mason-Dixon Line

they children | they children's children.
Come down with this. | pop-lock fever

Less than a generation | Everything but the Butterfly will be Pimped

Who mo' pretty than Muhammad Ali?
Your jembe is the Earth's museum

Steel Drum still sing us a symphony
of high-yellow blue-black and red-brown bees.

We was always the Buzz!

Your gospel it gon' grow wings
ubiquitous as Aretha's soundtrack

Beat up hard | cowhide drum
soul stripped stretched | cross barrel of gun.

TIME learned us her language;
Massa's rarest letters describe our JAZZ

A Global Discography run banshee
in the narrow grooves of that everlasting

round trip | of niggahs
ontopofniggahs | ontopof
niggahs on top | of niggahs

9.

Genius cannot be taught by repetition
discourse is Improvisation

tongue | depress | Insist
bend @ waist | open wide | Thrust

sundry dialects | blunt | cross your lips
Taste IT! | Their Jizz tastes nothing like JAZZ!

God's language unfolds a colony
boils a soul's transcriptase down to concentrate

sinks teeth down to marrow
Patois pulverizes to dust.

Inside lives whole bodies of living water.
Open up Buffalo Soldier.

An estuary riven with epigenetics
seed the farmlands they prepared

so well for Us. How else to catalogue
and dispense metric tons of cotton and chattel.

While God rocks his Fortune to the rhythm
of the blue-blue   black-black Sea

Music and matter, their primal mix, tracks
your progress through this dreary land.

God's People so immensely well-Chosen.
Our bodies break for you. Fill you to overflowing

with the brown blood of the Lamb.
History will never record a more weighty sacrifice.

10.

Remember

how you are remembered.

An ancestor's toast to you
their salt-water promise

Sellers of Universe beware.
TIME IS COMING for you to pay all your taxes

Niggahs never waited to be told we was being whipped
keloid canopy, read like braille, suffered the understanding for us!

never Did matter what the Massa-Prosecutor
down at Ferguson, Missouri's Little House
on the Prairie called it.

Firsthand, we had to name it correct.
When hands, any hands, is on a Niggah's throat

and they can't breathe, that Niggah is Being Choked.

never had no wait time
for no press conference

no court-martial
no 9 p.m. grand jury decision

Niggahs is experiential learners
Taught, over TIME, exact distance

alls our stories travel from the Truth.
We were and always have been

the God-damned evidence
left at the scene.

TIME   OUT!   THIS
SHIT   STOPS   HERE!

MOOD:
HERE FOR
THE
HEREAFTER

GLOSSOLALIA

An Etymology of a Scene
After "Necropolis" by Robert Vázquez-Pacheco

honey moon	**Fahiym Ratcliffe**	**Second 2 Last**	**Black Lotus**
bang zoom	**Iowan Tribal**	**SupaNova**	*S.L.OM.* **Entrfied**
Alice moon	**Thug Nubians** 452	**Burnt Sugar**	*mTkalla*
Nets Barclays	**Elton Leonard**	**Marco Jengkens**	**Aaron Simms**
Jay-Z's thick-lip brew	**Sacred Noise**	**Craig Knight**	**Derrick Cross**
Fulton tributary	**Anisa Fujah** *Dumeha Vernice*	**Ian Friday**	*Brian Polite*
eminent Dodgers' heartbreak	**Afro Mosaic Soul**	*Jah'Ni*	**Abhita**
Brooklyn thick-neck gazebo	**Aisha Tandiwe Bell**		*Regina Brooks*
nurse scalp bridge	**Tea Party Collective**	*Moshood*	**4W Circle**
word throat drum Nuyorican	**Eva Daniels**	**Courtney Washington**	
Nuyorican Nuyorican	**Terry & Tyrone Perkins**	*Brooklyn Moon Cafe*	
baked brown oil sun	**Night of the Cooker**	**Mike Thompson**	
will reconvene	*The Onliest* **Mrk Drkfthr**	*Survival Soundz*	
incense wrap	**Women in Love** *Bonafide*	**Miles Marshall Lewis**	
rehearsal rehearsal	**Greg Tate**	**Tureka Turk**	**Nzingha** **Folake**
Rehearse Its Universe	*Kevin Powell* **Jan** *Mshindo*	**Alexis Hightower**	
Rehearse rehearsals rehearse	**Sun Singleton**	**Shawn Banks**	
Erykah Mos's house	**Clayton Craddock**	*Chan Booth*	**Francesca**

house house house	**Yolan Sandy**	*Touch of Reality*	**Teabag**
party Bergen blowgun	**LuQuantum Leap**		*Micah BlackLight*
Nkiru Nkiru	**Brother Fred**	*Mandingo*	**Cleveland** *Sharon*
Nkiru larynx of stars	**E. Patrick Coker**	*Danielle*	**Thelma Emi**
blitzkrieg necklace	**Dwayne Rodgers**	**Lisa Manning**	*Tree*
Names: [Insert-sert	**Muhammad**	*Ray Bangs*	**Kecia Élan** *Christine*
-sert-sert] [In-In]	**Sharrif Simmons**	*Freedome Bradley*	**Mechelle (Self)**
[Insert]-[Insert] [Insert		*Kimberly Becoat*	**D.L. Hartley** **Joloff**
-ert] [Names Names]	**Pop** *Crash House*	**Kim Good**	*Cliff* **Mutale**
come came	**Eternal**	*Aleathia Brown*	**Mert Ogilvie** **Heather Keets**
come came	**Shannon** *Joy*	**Ruthie**	*Wil Hylton* **Deepalite** *Foote*
come came	**Carolyn A. Butts**	*African Voices*	**Reel Sisters**
Names kiss	*ImageNation*	**Gregory Gates**	*Moikgantsi Kgama*
paint praise	*Vashti* **D-MAX**	*Hakhi* **Ngoma**	*Aaqil* **Djibril**
joy joy joy	**Tjäde Graves**	*Three Bean Stew*	**Malik Yusef Cumbo**
joy Joy	**MB Singley**	**Ian Marquis**	*Ghana Imani* **Shani Gillespie**
Joy JOY	**Tyrone Francis**	*Amaris Moss*	**Shalewa Mackall** *Big Ron*
[insert]	**Imani Jones**	*Nyra* **Mia McLeod**	*Caroline Duvalsaint*
will will will	*Marco Sylla* **GRFX**	*Tantra*	**Mo Beasley** *Arlene Friday*
Joy joy sky		*Mrs. Friday* **Sydnee Stewart**	*UrbanErotika*
sky sky: mother	**Kwame Brandt-Pierce**	*Allison Bridges*	**Marie**
sand ship matter	*Medgar Evers*	**Carol's Daughter**	**Spike's Joint**
Brooklyn!	**Jamyla Bennu**	**Kia Shrine**	**Nathan Scott**

Under Noah Under   Ashaka Givens   *Everyanything*   Lorraine West

Noah Under Noah   Social Outcasts   Ainsley Burrows

ground ark train   Louis Reyes Rivera   *Tony Medina*

yard x. o. x. o. x. o.   asha bandele   Hattie Gossett   Bruce George

Ancestors. rust   Kyle Smith   Ebony Tynes   Niema Nteri Atkins

rinse   Isaiah Washington   Tehut-9   Rod McCoy   *Tracie Morris*

Afro-root new new   Dawoud Kringle   *Rakiem Walker*   Greg Purnell

new new mammon   *South Oxford Club*   Chris Eddleton   *LG*

remember?   Kamau   *N'dambi*   Khepra   *Mikel*   Fumi   *Nah'shon*

'member-member   Robbi   *D'Jahmu*   Nia Hamer   Nigel Barton

marrow real-time Refused   Ray Hands   Ron Trent   Little Ray

Liza Jessie Peterson   Carl Hancock Rux   Saul Williams

muMs the Schemer   *Carmen Renee Thompson*   Sol

Brad Walrond   *pierre bennu*   Kymbali Craig   *Suheir Hammad*

real-time Refused   Mos Def   *jessica Care moore*   Tish Benson

Shelley Nicole   *Universes*   Imani Uzuri   *Marcia Jones*   Juakali

Rha Goddess   LaTasha Natasha Diggs   *Sha-key*   Sarah Jones

Erykah Badu   Talib Kweli   Wood Harris   Francks Deceus

real-time   *Staceyann Chin*   Jasiri   *Danny Simmons*   Kayo

Refused   *Dawud Ruffin*   Sunday Tea Party   *Jamboree*

elf-slave magic.   Thoughtforms Underground   *Judson Church*

art   Del   *Raven*   Abiodun   *The Last Poets*   Michele Luc   *Paze*

brother-brother   yrteop   *The Point*   Nuyorican Poets Café

161

-brother exponent   **Afrikan Poetry Theatre**   *Coco Bar*   **Royston's**

genius reflex   **Brother Larry**   **Brother Wayne**   *Brother D*   **Leary**

reconfigure wind   **Diggs**   *Kim Knox*   **DeShawn Maxwell**

wry UBIQUITA   *DJ Reborn*   **DJ Selly**   *DJ Moni*   **Eric Spencer**

blunt-lip lit bodies-   *Vibe Chameleons*   **The Ladies of Ubiquita**

bodies-bodies Heineken   **Lisa** *Yvonne* **Joan** *Laura* **Gary Vidal**

Brooklyn Brooklyn   **Khadidjah**   *Lady Black*   **Shawn Alexander**

Brooklyn Promise remember   **Terrence Jennings**   **Erica Ford**

Stranger handy-handy man   **Sistas' Place**   *Mariahadessa Ekere* **Bade**

Remember? 'Member   **Maya** *Remileku* **Tamar-kali** *Honeychild*

'member promenade   **Sophia Ramos**   **Rob Fields**   *FunkFace*

audition   **Adia** *Meme* **Scott Wiley** *Alika Wade* **Stephen Miller**

giggles door language   **Luqman Brown**   *Ramsey Jones*   **Greer**

loss Brooklyn   **Jerome Jordan**   **Corey Glover**   **Leah Bennet**

getting over   **Vernon Reid**   *Black Rock Coalition*   **Alvin Seme**

prevail laugh   **Mabili Kregg**   **Ajamu**   *Darrell McNeill*

hoist   **Mildred Ruiz**   **Steven Sapp**   *Flaco*   **Lemon Anderson**

reconvene   *Gamal Chasten*   **Queen Afua**   *Ankhman*   **Troy Pennerman**

[insert]   **After Life**   **Kim Lightfoot**   *Kalim Shabazz*   **Nana Ataa**

[your]   *Body & Soul*   **Joe Claussell**   *Danny Krivit*   **François Kevorkian**

wingspan ship kiss   **Ian Rock**   *Sound Factory Bar*   **Louie Vega**

beget crush glide pieces   *Barbara Tucker*   **Willi Ninja**   *Martine*

[name name name]   **Shelter**   *Timmy Regisford*   **Mother Earth** [name name] [here]   **Serge**   *Behind Club Doors*   **Manski**

BROOKLYN!   **Cherise Trahan**   **Keith Chandler**   *Vilma*

MULTI VERSE   *DJ Basil*   **Octagon**   **Warehouse**   **Fred Pierce**

[INSERT]   **SOB's**   *Krash*   **Two Potato**   *DJ Andre Collins*

[insert insert] [your name here]   **James Saunders**   **Clubhouse**

past unrequited   **Baby Jupiter**   *Brownies*   **Alafia Hampden**

its uni verse   *Wetlands*   **One Hot Spot**   **Jason Scott Jones**

gales home   **Café con Leche**   *Milk Mondays*   **Dance Tracks**

Pep Zook MC   **DJ Merritt**   *Esquelita*   **SUSPECT**   **Brown Hornet**

[INSERT] [YOUR NAME]   *DJ Unknown*   **Keller's**   **Vinylmania**

Zake gone   *Rebel Rebel*   **Lenox Lounge**   *Adana Hylton*

Queen   **Nate & Fernando**   *Steph Wiley*   **Jose Ivey**

homage weep   **Yarnell**   *Carlos Omar Gardinet*   **Bardeaux**

phrase rainbow   **The Lab**   *667*   **Pink Tea Cup**   *Osandu*

Zoom moon   *Litina Egungun*   **Yvette Ganier**   **Carlos Sanchez**

Alice hole black   **Junior Vasquez**   *Rockwell's*   **Langston's**

hole black hole   **No Parking**   *Shark Bar*   **Mecca**   *Freedom Rag*

whole whole whole black   **Mahess Bennett**   *Ambessa*   **Lisa Bennett**

black Black Brooklyn   **Ellehcem Hutchinson**   *Dawn Norfleet*

Universe STARS!   **Victoria**   **Jonathan and Joseph Baston**

[HERE!]   **Frankie Paradise**   *M Kayana Lewis*   **Kelli Curtis**

RARE EARTH   NEW EARTH

A Contrapuntal

gene code so fluid | life course corrects everything
everyone still born different | blow hard enough become the wish
enough to be a witness | most deviance is the art of being
party to one's own deliverance. | an original.

Live your Myth | placeholders trap themselves
unfollow everyone else | algorithms chase their placebos with poison.
mills prescribe their omens | we all worship something
memes addict to the following | guns, snake oil, dead presidents

home grown forms of terror | all the nouns have triggers
consumption and slave labor | this country shoots the
present can't be always | generous. Futures count the balance
how we land inside a chalk outline | nothing left right to see here

Buck the list! | leave the billionaires
Life still out there somewhere | Let them crash-course some new Earth
play the remix. | We are the rare Earths

we've been waiting for.

164

CYBORG HEAVEN

After Alberto Pereira Jr.

How might a poem ever be entered
If one insists on living outside of it

As if truth ever estranges from its confession.
shut off, attenuated—severed even—from the silence

hoping for a quiet burial of its secrets
inside the belly of a thing

—is a body

                Touch.
                touch It

The crushed, frot grape,
The burst skin of an opened chalice

The ferment lust routed toward its own becoming
a swallowed, a delectable, an abusable thing.

Plain as evidence: how hickeys cum first, leave secondhand.
Mapping, in an instant, the truancy of the desired

and its bruised consequence. the Possessed remind of
their dispossession. the lover, the scorned, incite

the tangled algorithms to their dangled,
nonlocal dance of the Survived.

> *Touch*
> *touch me here*

COVID-19 | 80s come HIV
2020, unspell the undercount of
the infected and the unbelieved.

a mirror referees the chupacabra
apart from its chimeric twin

still haunting the olde AIDS mausoleum.

Toggling between: | pixel + time | betwixt | Java + Script |

New Worlds project into and out of the
digital forest where screens screen now
as much for the troll as the Corona;

the drone | the android | the Teletubby

as much as the quarantined.

> *Here in Cyborg Heaven where we are all only fans*

of the fatte | the femme | the nanosex
the trans | the zaddy | the cougar | the bear,

the intersex and the polyamorous.
the non-binary codes of the sapio-sanct,

pan the bisexual algorithms of the marooned

Here where apples and operating systems bear less and less fruit

more and more seed spill
into isolate and heartache.

pills pop, crystals smoke the anxious and the paranoid
into novel forms of forgiveness and the unforgiven

Every one hides behind an Instagram scene

pandemics push portals onto the outcast fringe
of the human condition. Shame and stigma snag

right where the shunned escape,
battered and bruised into their ennui Underground

Every box signals a beginning

of a turn | a twist | an impulse
a tremor | an anguish | a horned head

a taut arm | a whetted hand |
whistle the opened organ called to task

the hardening fruit of the willing and the wild.
The Object is to get inside, beside, beneath it, get into it!

Test how the right entrance can make
as much noise as the Entered.

Touch | touch | touch | touch-touch | touch it!
every crevice | every ending | objects to nothing

Zoom in, magnify how salt, pearl, water exudes for you
behind the glass | in front the screen | in opened air.

Don't it move you into your want?:
emulsify | trigger | reflex | unfold before intent

    Attends to any theory of mind

Touch | touch | touch me please
I am it | and it is not me

Blood belongs and un-belongs
to the viral | the virile | the vile

The live stream clings and un-clings to the
breathy contour of its own ecstatic perdition.

Tunnels | tides | tubes swell their miasmas into
the surrounded air. Our insides bare the implicit need

to be touched | to be held | to be nursed,
by the enveloped suck of hot tongue and recycled wind.

    Touch me | touch me | Touch me | please

The boxed | the unboxed
The bruised | the belonged

The looked-over | the overlooked
the puddle | the oasis | the pond.

The breeding ground for the succumbed
and the spawned | the required | the acquired

the healed | the traumatized | the fixed | the fixated
The errand boy | the homing pigeon | The prodigal | and the returned

We are what else besides a meeting ground:

Heart   body   fluid   mind
Touch me PLeasseee!!!

Where mask nor rubber can withstand the cover
of this blood-borne anointing.

Laced to my sins | my heart | my obsessions
my endeavors | my crimes | my longings.

Received | endowed | and pressed into Beings like me.
Touch us please!

The infected | affected | the unadorned and the adored.
Here every transgression belies the confectioned underbelly

to every sacral push and insists we hold on
and hold out for some thing, any thing
holy | warmed | and Divine (d).

#ₐMOOD

After The Beneficiaries *by Jeff Mills & jessica Care moore*

Color every body. What colors have you now?
a planetarium, a cathedral, an inner sanctum,
  an uninhibited planet. What color are you?

Imagine all the futures have passed. Story,
outlives the eternal Gods here to shame
A *Kidd*, in a strange city, lost inside a poem.

I imagine rare views are everywhere.
The black hole had to be felled on top us.
The Species did not fall willing prey.

In fact & fiction *IQ84* and *Dhalgren* share a 2nd moon.
In the obscured bed of supermassive visionaries,
black experiment uniquely indwells the

vessel, the spaceship, the denied
conscience. The satellite, the Covenant
managing man's disquiet inside

future and the past. deconstructs reconstructs the
the sacred pact. Curiosity is the survivable Heaven
a hungry indefatigable question:

its own genome. We suck chew and bleed;
as if we all belonged to the crushed paint.
At the opened gamete, our nano blooms.

blood will always be part of the story?
The kind that courts the moon. The human surf
in waste pursuit of owning space and

New clothes. Dimensions swarm
without excuse or equivalence
The fiber optics infuse what was left

form. Poets don't always survive the hard lesson
words are extra ordinary free and costly things.
Promise to leave at least one poem

for the dead. The forgotten Angel
patent in our bone.
After that too olde century

that wrote itself into existence
In all possible futures
a human heart remains the mystery.

Under someone else's warden, *Tengo, Aomame* eclipse their own fate.
Hegemony discard their dead plastic Novel beginnings are everywhere
toy soldiers masquerade. Privilege is, in the end, a cowardice

A learning disability portends a city's collapse
New skins drip outside our turtled shells. Kidds come and go
Outside the hard-luck wall as they please. without names,

We are opened, we are closed in without fathers, without shoes
Tidy boundaries lose their utility in at least one universe
In hyperspace. All our colors dissolve. the children remind us

We are no longer colors. Our homes are scarce hard-won places
Empath harvests. Nuclei & hormone. An Orchid, an Air Chrysalis
Cyborg and Organelle. Make of us so much

a mood. A Heaven we can all hold more than we seem
In our hand; Closed eyes, opened hungry curious hearts weigh

The body's rite to *Lucy's* light
lucid dream.

AMPHIBIA

After Kahlil Joseph's short film Black Mary, *featuring Alice Smith*

> *I put a spell on you;*

This grooved soprano a saline well.
The ghosts sanctify in sackcloth and ash,
patient as dolls, swaying, in cipher, holding court,

holding breath, waiting for the services to begin.
The water is always troubled here;
Somebody's some body always falling in.

Something wet, swole, Brown, tilled,
must encourage the bodies through to the other side.
Amphibia is the only pre-condition answered in black prayer.

> *I put a spell on you*

There is a bayou swum in broken bones.
This kind of snatching only returns bloated things.
It is not that we are well. Rather, we've found a way to nurse

the only water source in the wail of the unpronounced.
History half-erect inside these walls, swells into an Abstract.
Grabs at the throat—any throat —it can find.

A shrill anoints at the half measure, curdles at half control.
Psalm oil shook wild as the Beginnings of any thing
formed of too many worlds.

> *Whatever it is, it —it won't let me—*
> *Ho-o-old my peace.*

It has already survived the demise,
the burden, the betrayal,
the selling away, of all one's beloved.

> *I put a spell on you*   *—Whatever it is—*   *it won't let me*

All other life *still* yet spawn from here:
that pitch, that soot, that ink, that Blues,
that din, that dusk, that sink, that brood

is-is that which had no way to be Enough.
And-too, is-is that which could not have ever been
Enough. Is-is that which would require

all surrender of need. To scout out
that which might could hold the prophet
inside the promise

> of more-more-more-more-more than Enough.

That terra firma, that countertenor. That-that which
—*Whatever it is*— must needs be all that there ever was.
All that there ever must will ever be.

the Trouble?

—Here in the absence of all else—

Planets drown. The undead float
inside the terrors of a whole world

Breonna Taylor died again today,
Slipping through our arms

      she's mine! She's mine.
      she was mine-mine.   *She was mine*

      i put a spell on you;

A cry, for one mortal, cannot sound like this.
This sound—the stretch of it—strains into the
fissure at the river's edge.

This half soprano, half railroad,
half voice-over, half afterbirth,
must be the last early warning siren.

EPILOGUE.

INSIDE THIS GIF

Conscious lives die inside this GIF
Consciousness lives dies inside this GIF
Conscious lives die inside this GIF

Resistance is fertile

Mankind is the Dinosaur we rode to extinction

#selfies discover their vulgar pointlessness

The Individual is an artifact

The Apocalypse goes viral

Forgiveness, the One we called

When Darwin's childhood definitions had finally failed

The speed of light is reached @ Consciousness

We Babel again

The Great Pyramid of Giza was built by 3-D Printers!

Even @ singularity the matrix cannot program itself

Science too will beg us for a metaphysics

Resistance is Fertile

Where is maya now?

Where are the Maya?

History had too many Reservations

Man's greatest folly is to think

We All-Stars and non-binaries

The proof of God is the proliferation of Demons

Natural selection is jargon

Creation is a much more beautiful word

God never got Religion

Resistance is fertile

The European Unifies What?

Gibraltar no longer bears weight

Has any one living heard of NATO?

Resistance is fertile

There are no Virgins in the Space Tourism business

Do you remember when?

The Tennessee Legislature was not a slave state?

When I go to the hospital, I talk to the nurses

They remember the Gods the Doctors long since forgot

God's tag name is: Consciousness

Infinity is Heaven and Hell without borders

War on Terror is a tautology

Most Intelligence is bad

Quantum leaps jumped us

White supremacists are granted no immunity

For their apparent success in the preceding round

Irony is the divine principle

How else is consciousness remained?

Equal parts everywhere

Every where alien

Only our devolution will save us now

Ashes to Ashes

Dust to Democracy

Resistance is fertile

Conscious lives die inside this GIF
Consciousness lives dies inside this GIF
Conscious lives die inside this GIF

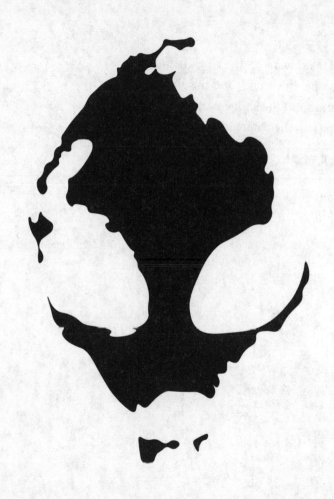

"Because that means it's the city. That means it's the landscape: the bricks, and the girders, and the faulty wiring and the shot elevator machinery, all conspiring together to make these myths true."

—SAMUEL R. DELANY

Notes

The opening epigraph is taken from W. E. B. Du Bois, *The Philadelphia Negro: A Social Study* (1899; reis., New York: Oxford University Press, 2007), 269–270.

PROLOGUE.

In "The Untitled, the Unnamed, & the Unnameable," the first quote is from John Franklin Jameson, *Narratives of New Netherland, 1609–1664* (New York: C. Scribner's Sons, 1909), 259–260. The second quote is from *Narratives of New Netherland*, 262.

GOTHAM: WHERE THE KIDS RAISE THEMSELVES

In "Pablo the Afrofuturist: Anyanwu Takes Over Picasso's Tumblr Feed," I asked graphic designer Tim Nottage to create a near facsimile of one of the black-and-white paintings from *Picasso Black and White* (New York's Solomon R. Guggenheim Museum's 2012–2013 debut exhibition exploring Picasso's remarkable use of black and white throughout his career).

The aim here is to visually depict in real time the subject of the poem—the co-opting of an artist's work and artistic tradition without adequate attribution. In the end, we chose to recreate and transform Picasso's *Head of a Woman* drawing from his extensive War and Peace series of the early 1950s.

HOME CHURCH: HOW HOUSE MAKES A HOME

The poem "For Marjory: A Tribute" is written to honor the life and legacy of Marjory Smarth, renowned dancer, teacher, and cultural ambassador of New York City's underground dance music community.

In "Swag on Fleek: World Is a Ghetto (Rehearsal Version)," the bolded text on the right side comprise a poem of their own. Each line is a track from War's fifth album, *The World Is a Ghetto*, released in 1972 by Far Out Records.

For a deeper context of the history chronicled in "1986: An Elegy for Our Coldest War," a complete indexed version prepared by Robert Sember can be found at https://urldefense.com/v3/__https://www.artseverywhere.ca/1986/__;!!FOS tn7g!FUzQvVfWbg3lztKaq6W5IEe2eh-R6yYVNKtH22fhgAE1zsTwYF rANOa-on2eGSHQfJ3bi_NHCrlaaAjs4s-Ad0p6XvcO$ https://www.artsevery where.ca/1986/.

MANHOOD: A BOY'S CALCULUS

In "Kanyechukwuekele: 'Let's Give God Praise,'" I make references to the Igbo pantheon. *Chukwu* is the supreme being and is represented by the sun. *Chineke* is the creator of the world and nature. *Chi* is a subdeity akin to a personal spiritual guide. *Ala* refers to the individual human spirit or soul.

Maafa is a Swahili term meaning "great disaster," introduced by Marimba Ani's book *Let the Circle Be Unbroken: The Implications of African Spirituality in the Diaspora*, as per Nah Dove, *Afrikan Mothers: Bearers of Culture, Makers of Social Change* (Albany, NY: SUNY Press, 1998), 240.

"They Crowned Him: An Elegy to Kalief Browder," as originally published in africanvoices.com, was written in the weeks following Kalief Browder's death.

The data points in the poem reflect the published information surrounding his biography and ordeal at the time. Since then, *The New Yorker* issued a correction indicating Kalief used bedsheets attached to the air-conditioning unit to end his life.

Each of the (4) contrapuntal poems in this work—the "Autocorrect: Dear John, Revelation 1:14–15" poem; the "Autocorrect: The Ayahuasca Remix" poem; the "Rare Earth New Earth" poem; and the "#AMood" poem—can be read as four distinct poems in one: each of the two poems reads horizontally from left to right, line by line, as one poem; the left column reads vertically as its own separate poem; the right column reads vertically as its own separate poem; and together, the left and right columns read vertically, line by line, as their own poem.

MOOD: HERE FOR THE HEREAFTER

The format for "Glossolalia: An Etymology of a Scene" is inspired by Robert Vázquez-Pacheco's poem "Necropolis" in *Sojourner: Black Gay Voices in the Age of AIDS*, ed. B. Michael Hunter (New York: Other Countries Press, New York, 1993), 25.

In "Necropolis," Vázquez-Pacheco memorializes, in the right margin, the names of friends, lovers, fellow writers, acquaintances the Other Countries collective had lost to HIV/AIDS in the years between the publishing of volume I and volume II. "Necropolis" shows us what it feels like to exist as a survivor in a city of ghosts.

"Glossolalia: An Etymology of a Scene" is a deconstruction of "Barclays Center: The Day Before the Day After Tomorrow" earlier in this work. "Glossolalia" celebrates many of the names (living and transitioned) of the artists, beings, venues, bands, musicians, collectives that comprised the overlapping New York City–based poetry, spoken word, visual art, black gay/queer artivist, black rock/alternative music, underground dance, and house music scenes, each of which served as feeder lines to what would later be called the New Black Arts Movement.

The closing epigraph is taken from Samuel R. Delany, *Dhalgren* (1974; reis., New York: Vintage Books, 2001), 249.

Acknowledgments

A multitude is responsible for this book's birth. Thank you Toni Asante Light-foot, for being the first to take an immersive critical look. Your keen and sha-manic aesthete singularly helped to eke a sacred, standard-bearing foundation for these poems. You lent this writer the surest footing to reach for the stars. Poet, friend, comrade Joel Francois, thank you for being the capstone eye on this project. Your extreme talent and care bloomed these poems out of their final trenches. I have not enough praise for your heart-willed endurance. Shel-ley Nicole Jefferson for your love and friendship; there are so many ways I could never say thanks. Thank you for bejeweling *Every Where Alien* with your high-holy spit shine. Your life work, cultural memory, eye for detail, and drill-down persistence have helped this work showcase with fidelity the spirit, art, artists, and institutions of the New Black Arts Movement. Tim Nottage, thank you for your immeasurable and important contribution to *Every Where Alien*. You have so ably translated the layers of this project into legible and brilliant design.

Upon returning to my craft, untold individuals and institutions have made room for my voice and praxis. Thank you, *African Voices Magazine*, for pub-lishing "They Crowned Him: An Elegy to Kalief Browder" and "Zake." Thank you, Carolyn A. Butts, for your global-art-amplifying vision and light. Thank you, Michael Roberson, Robert Sember, and the Arbert Santana Ballroom Freedom and Free School, for publishing "1986: An Elegy for Our Coldest War" as a textbook. Thank you, Dr. Jennifer Lee and #houselivesmatter, for supporting and nurturing my work with the house ballroom community both here in New York City and in São Paulo, Brazil. Icon Pony Zion, thank you for the mercy and grace you extend this artist, and for your leadership of the International House of Zion. Thank you, Luv t'il it hurts, for supporting the expansion of this work to São Paulo, Brazil. Thank you, Other Countries, for receiving my itinerant self with open arms to workshop some of the poems here. Thank you, Poem-a-Day | Academy of American Poets, Honorée Fanonne Jeffers, ArtsEverywhere, *Moko Magazine, Eleven Eleven, Wordpeace, About Place Journal,* and *Taint Taint Taint Literary Magazine* for publishing my work.

Thank you, Vince Boudreau, my friend, mentor, and thirteenth president of The City College of New York, for your catalytic and everlasting impact on my mind and craft. Thank you, Dee Dee Mozeleski and The City College family, for all the prescient ways an alma mater nurses its own. Thank you, CW Integrity Solutions. Thank you, Ian Friday and the global Sunday Tea Party family. Ian, your quiet genius and brotherhood make this artist way worthwhile. Tish Benson, thank you for our intergalactic communion. Thank you, Kimberly Becoat, Shreya Mandal, Kim Knox, Steven A. Williams, for your love, art, work ethic, inspiration, and activist witness.

Special thanks to my partner, Julius Jerome Powell. This artist simply does not exist without your love and support. I thank my family, colleagues, and friends for your continued support. To Lekule, despite appearances, I will surely require a lifetime of our friendship. Davy, ever, ever, ever thanks. Thank you, Joey Pressley and Steven A. Williams, for never not being there. Colin Robinson, thank you for being an artivist beacon for the black queer diaspora. Your outsized courage and visionary lifework endure as a portal marshaling our collective agency and our individual service.

Deep thanks to my editor Francesca Walker and the entire team at Harper-Collins. Regina Brooks, my friend and literary agent, thank you for singularly being an anchor and an under-ground highway. jessica Care moore, your friendship is how I breathe. Your commitment to poems, activism, art, and artists is a force field wrapped around the whole world. Thank you, Moore Black Press, for believing in this work before it had a name or a voice of its own. Your faith and commitment to *Every Where Alien* has been its most reliable, boundless, sustainable fuel source.

Finally and forever, thank you, Ntozake Shange, for whispering in my ear, "Brad, your audience is waiting for you." Zake, you remain for me and so many: the reason!

About the Author

Brad Walrond's debut collection, *Every Where Alien*, is published by Moore Black Press. The themes here explore the author's own black queer exploration of the world, domestic and abroad, and how these experiences map onto the discovery of co-occurring and overlapping art and resistance movements among New York City's underground communities—communities like the New Black Arts Movement, the New York ballroom scene, the Black Rock Coalition, the underground house dance and music community, and the black queer political arts and activist movements that arose in response to racism, homophobia, transphobia, and the HIV/AIDS pandemic.

Poet, author, mixed-media performance artist, and activist Brad Walrond is a graduate of The City College of New York and earned his MA degree in political science from Columbia University. His poetics, performance, and multidisciplinary work span the nexus between virtual reality, identity formation, and human consciousness at the intersection of race, gender, sex, and desire. Brad was born in Brooklyn, New York, to first-generation parents from Barbados. He began writing and performing at the age of twenty-four when he was commissioned to participate in a theatre production keynoted by Harry Belafonte, and he soon became one of the foremost writers and performers of the 1990s Black Arts Movement centered in New York City. With his work, Brad crafts new portraiture that radically reimagines our shared human inheritance and how our pasts and futures make more space for performances of justice and joy. His poetics and praxis have taken him across the country and as far as São Paulo, Brazil, and Taipei, Taiwan.

www.bradwalrond.com